Shoujoai ni Bouken:
The Adventures of Yuriko

Written by Erica Friedman
Illustrated by Kelli Nicely

ISBN 0-9759160-2-5

Author's Note

In 2000, after years of wasting time reading comic books and watching cartoons, I became the unlikely founder of an online organization called Yuricon. Yuricon's stated mission was to bring together fans of Japanese animation and comics that focused specifically on lesbian characters and stories (a genre we call *Yuri*). Yuricon was created half as a joke, half with a genuine mission - I'd like to think that we've managed to maintain both these things over the past years and have never taken ourselves *too* seriously, while also keeping our focus.

Because Yuricon was meant to be by lesbians, for lesbians (although we have always welcomed anyone, male or female, who wanted to join us online or at our events) I wanted our mascot to be unique - someone who reflected our ideal manga character. And so Yuriko, the out, lesbian, Japanese pop idol, was born.

By making Yuriko a pop idol, I could pretty much do *anything* with her and make it plausible - a great advantage for a writer who loves to write the improbable, as long as it is even remotely plausible. It's a perfect set-up.

Once I knew who our mascot was, I wanted very much to introduce her to the rest of the world. *Shoujoai ni Bouken* was originally written as a "fan fiction" for Yuriko. I thought long and hard about what kind of fanfic I wanted to write for Yuriko and I decided that the only fitting thing would be to give her a *shoujo manga* (Japanese for "girls' comic") of her own. Unfortunately, I can't draw a straight line with a ruler, so manga was out. So, instead, I wrote a serialized novel. This story was originally distributed twice a week in short serial "issues" on the Yuricon Mailing List. It was

i

intended to be read one chapter at a time, not in one long marathon. As a result, it may seem a little choppy if you read it all at once. I have left the volume and issue numbers intact, but I have removed "The Story So Far" inserts that initially prefaced each chapter.

I wanted *Shoujoai ni Bouken* to read like a shoujo manga, with all the requisite love complications and the usual high school setting, but I also wanted it to be something more - a story of a lesbian who was happy with herself and her life. Yuriko is a woman who isn't coming out or hiding her sexual preference, but neither is she wrapped up in her gay identity to the exclusion of everything else. In effect, the kind of person I think we should all be able to be. Both the fulltext of this novel, and the current chapters of the sequel, *Saiyuu no Ryokou*, are available online on the Yuricon website. You're very welcome to visit the site and enjoy the rest of the story!

There may be words and concepts strange to readers who are not familiar with the conventions of Japanese manga or culture. I sincerely hope that most of these terms will be self-explanatory, or will be understandable in context. If not, I guess I'll just nip off and shoot myself, since that would mean I'm a failure as a writer. To avoid this outcome, I have added a Glossary of Terms and Concepts at the back of the book.

I'd like to take a moment to thank some people: The Fanfic Revolution, my dear friends and excellent editors; Erin Subranamian for her invaluable advice on the Glossary; the members of Yuricon, whose support for and interest in Yuriko's adventures have kept this story alive for me long after it was completed; Editor Ed and all the staff at Yuricon and ALC Publishing. Kelli for her wonderful illustrations and her even better backrubs. And as always, I want to thank my Muse, my wife, and my love, who all happen to be the same person.

- Erica Friedman, February 2005

Yuricon - "For real women who love their women...animated."
http://www.yuricon.org

Shoujoai ni Bouken

Illustrated by | Kelli Nicely

ALC Editing Staff | Ed Chapman
Janice Marcus

Production Editor | Paulette Hodge

Publisher | Erica Friedman

Special Thanks | Bruce Pregger
Zeyl

Email: anilesbocon01@hotmail.com
www.anilesbocon.org/alc.htm

ALC Publishing

Meet Yuriko

"Just once more and we're done." Yuriko could feel the cool slime of cold cream pass across her cheek, followed by a vigorous circular rubbing motion. Her skin became warm, and the slimy feeling changed to a slightly tacky sensation. She sighed impatiently and crossed her arms. The sensation ceased.

"You're done." The hairdresser was tall, scandalously thin and exceptionally effeminate. He put his hands on his hips and looked at Yuriko condescendingly. "That wasn't *that* bad, was it?" He leaned forward, peering at her closely. "Oh wait, I missed…" She slapped his hand away and stood abruptly.

"That's it! I'm done here! Sheesh!" Yuriko ripped the smock from around her neck. "Thanks, sweetie, but I have to go home." She slammed the smock down onto the chair she had vacated and was at the door in three steps.

As she left the room, she could hear the hairdresser saying petulantly, "Fine, but don't complain to me if you have dry skin!" Yuriko bared her teeth in what might have passed for a smile and slammed the door. Stopping in the hall, she sagged back against the wall and took a deep breath.

A woman laughed, the voice musical and girlish. "Yuri-chan, did the widdle hairdwessers abuse you again?" Yuriko looked up to see her best friend, Mariko, waiting for her.

Yuriko smiled and straightened. "Yes, they're really too much. In fact," she gestured broadly, "this is all insanely over the top. It's only a commercial, for pity's sake, not that you'd know it from the way André is acting." She caught up to Mariko and the two women started down the hallway. "I mean, we've been filming for three days already!"

Mariko laughed again. "You are such a whiner, Yuri. Most women in your position would be thrilled."

"I'm not most women," Yuriko commented unnecessarily.

Glancing up at her friend, Mariko enquired, "You seem in a rush. Got another date tonight?"

Grinning sardonically, Yuriko shook her head. "No. I'm beat…I think I'll just go straight home tonight."

Mariko watched her for a moment then stopped where she stood. Pointing at Yuriko, she laughed behind her hand. "You didn't get any offers today, did you?"

Yuriko looked down at her friend, startled, then flushed slightly. "No, as a matter of fact."

Mariko leaned against the wall, almost doubled over with laughter. "Poor, Yuri. How are you going to stand it…after all, you've got needs," she giggled, until Yuriko closed in on her, pinning her to the wall.

Yuriko glared down at her friend, and bared her teeth once again. "I guess I'll just have to rely on my friends, then…" She leaned forward, moving her face close to Mariko's.

Mariko gasped, then blushed, then flushed dark red and pushed Yuriko away. "No! I can't…wait, that's not what I meant…" she stammered as she realized that Yuriko was laughing at her. She turned away angrily and began walking down the hall again. She could hear Yuriko catch up, but ignored her.

"Sorry," Yuriko apologized.

Mariko softened, then smiled. "It's okay - after all, I was teasing you first." She paused. "You didn't mean it, right?" she asked softly.

Yuriko took Mariko's arm and threaded it through her own. "It depends." Mariko turned to look at her friend, open-mouthed, then realizing that Yuriko was still teasing her, slapped the blonde with her free hand.

Laughing, the two women left the studio.

***

"Ladies and Gentleman, I'd like you all to welcome the hottest thing to come down the pike this week...Yuriko!" *Ouch, that hurts*

Applause, teenyboppers screaming.

"Welcome, Yuriko…thanks for coming."

"Thanks for having me."

Mutual bowing, shaking hands, sitting.

"Wow - I see you've got quite a fan club here." Laughter.

Shy smile. "I can't help it, apparently." More laughter, more screams.

"Well, let's see - you're doing modeling right now, right?"

"Ah, yes. I have a new series of commercials coming out. We just finished filming them. Um, they'll be on the air in a month or so."

"What our viewers really want to know, Yuriko, is about you, personally. Do you have any hobbies?"

Cross legs, place hands on knee. "I like to dance." Screams interrupt. Wave at fans a little, grinning.

"Your fans seem to know that already." Chuckling.

Look down at paper. "How about boyfriends? Anyone special in your life right now?"

Grin, look into the camera, "There's no one special person right now…or a boyfriend, either." Screams again, increasing in volume. Nervous laughter from the host.

"Let's see…at twenty-four you've already made a name for yourself in music, modeling and acting. What's next for you?"

Hand behind head, look embarrassed. "I'm not really sure. Another acting role, if a good one comes along…maybe a new album. I guess we'll see."

The host nods, catches the signal for commercial. "Well, thanks for coming by today - everybody, let's hear it for Yuriko!" Gesture, applause, shrieks. Stand, shake hands, bow. Host turns away, looking a little discomfited. Walk off stage, grinning.

At the back door, fangirls press up against the barrier. Lean over, place a kiss on one cheek, press another hand, sign a few autographs. One little girl, all brown eyes and nervousness, passes over a rose. Break the stem, tuck the rose into lapel, then slowly, carefully, kiss the back of her hand. Watch as she nearly passes out and her friends practically climb over the barrier.

With a wave and a smile, climb into the car. Lean back and loosen the tie. Heavy sigh. One more down, only a thousand to go.

***

"Yuri, do you have any white wine?" Mariko asked, her head buried in the refrigerator.

"Check in the rack."

"I did - there isn't any."

"You are a such a pain sometimes." Yuriko turned on the CD player, then

Name: Yuriko

Birthday: February 22

Zodiac Sign: Pisces

Blood Type: O

Occupation: Pop Idol, Singer, Actress, Model

Favorite Color: Red

Favorite Food: Italian, Miso Soup

Favorite Music: Cello Concertos

Least Favorite Thing: Cooking

stepped towards the kitchen. She opened the closet, dug her way into the back and pulled out a bottle with a bow tied to its neck. Mari took it from her and smiled at the bow. Soft strains of a cello concerto filled the apartment.

"Gift from another admirer?"

"Mari!" Yuriko snapped. "You are bad…. No, a gift from a friend, if you must know."

Mari chuckled and opened the bottle. She poured two glasses and handed one over to Yuriko, who sipped at it.

The two women sat comfortably, without unnecessary chatter. Mariko watched her friend recline on the sofa, eyes closed. Her lean form was complimented by the suit she wore, the tie insouciantly loose, her gold wire-rim glasses giving her an academic look. She looked like a young college professor from a novel, Mariko thought. The kind that is always having advances made towards him by the students.

Without opening her eyes Yuriko asked, "You seeing Hachi tonight?" Mari swallowed her wine and placed the glass on the table at her side.

"Yes, he's coming here to pick me up - is that okay?"

"Oh, sure." Yuriko sipped more of her wine. "What time is he coming?"

Mariko raised an eyebrow. "What time do you need me gone?"

Yuriko's eyes opened and she gave Mariko an innocent stare. "I don't know what you mean."

"When is she coming?" Mari choked on her words as soon as she said them. "I mean, when is she supposed to be here?"

Yuriko gave her friend a wry grin. "About eight."

"Checking my date out?" Yuriko laughed.

"You know I'm always looking out for you."

"Always. You're the best, Mari." Yuriko leaned forward and held her glass out. Mariko tapped hers against Yuriko's and they both drank.

The doorbell rang at 7:55; Mariko got up to answer it. Her fiancé, Hachigoro, gave her a smile and entered, kissing her shyly on the cheek. Waving past Mariko at Yuriko, Hachi stepped up into the apartment. "I hope we're not being too inconvenient," Hachi said, his voice almost soft enough to cover his slight lisp.

Mari slipped her arm through his. "We have to go…in a few."

Hachi laughed in Yuriko's direction. "Got a hot date tonight?" He slipped an arm around Mari and looked at her fondly. "Me too."

Mari slapped his arm lightly. "You hope."

Yuriko grinned at her friends. "Yeah, me too." They all laughed.

The doorbell rang again. Yuriko jumped up from the sofa. "If it's alright with you, I'll get this one." She opened the door to a petite woman whose short, dark hair swung lightly at her temples. She was wearing a short Chinese-style dress that on another woman might have looked flashy - on her it looked natural. She bowed slightly to Yuriko and stepped into the foyer. Glancing up, she was surprised to see Hachi and Mari.

"Uh," Hachi said hastily, "we have to be going."

Yuriko closed the door and introduced her friends to her date. "This is Faye. She's from Hong Kong."

Greetings were made, then Mari grabbed Hachi's arm. "We really have to be going now."

Yuriko waved brightly as Mari winked behind Faye's head. The door closed once again.

***

"So, how was Faye?" Mariko asked the next day. Yuriko sat in her trailer, waiting for the camera call.

"You mean how was my date with her, don't you?" Yuriko asked pointedly, glaring as best she could without cracking the makeup on her face. She was dressed as an Edo-period samurai, with almost Kabuki-like heavy white makeup lying thickly on her face.

"No." Mariko said lightly.

"You're really twisted, you know?"

"Hachi and I thought she was cute." Mari continued as if the blonde hadn't spoken.

"Me too." Yuriko grinned, then immediately thought better of it.

***

The door shut behind Yuriko. She walked over to the desk and seated herself on the corner, grinning down at the harried form of her manager.

"Get off my desk." The cigarette dangling from Kishi's mouth punctuated her comments by wagging up and down as she spoke.

Yuriko didn't move. "Your chairs are uncomfortable."

"Then sit on the floor...or stand. Get your butt off my desk." Kishi looked up and glared.

Yuriko stood, laughing. "Okay, okay." She held up her hands placatingly and backed away from the desk. Seating herself in one of the chairs, Yuriko put her hands behind her head and lounged while her manager pointedly ignored her.

At last the older woman pushed the papers on her desk aside. Taking a deep drag from her cigarette, she blew out the smoke and ground the stub out.

"So," she said, giving Yuriko an acid look. "Where the *hell* have you been? I've been calling you for two days!" Kishi slammed her hand on the desk in frustration.

Yuriko's slow smile was maddening. "At a *love hotel*."

Kishi sneered. "Uh-huh." She reached for a pack of cigarettes and lit a new one. "For two days."

Yuriko's smile broadened. "Yup."

"Gods," Kishi muttered, "you are such a…"

"Tomcat," a male voice interceded neatly. The owner of the voice entered from the front door and bowed slightly to Yuriko.

Kishi sucked on the cigarette, but said nothing further. Yuriko bounced to her feet and bowed deeply.

"Good afternoon, Miyamoto-san." Yuriko could be charming when she wanted, Kishi admitted to herself, but the girl really got on her last nerve.

"Good afternoon, Yuri-kun, Kishi-san." The agency manager beamed at them. "We've just got news of a great new opportunity for you, Yuri-kun." He handed over a sheaf of papers to the manager, who ground out her finished cigarette and leaned over the desk to receive them.

Yuriko nodded. "What kind of opportunity?"

Miyamoto smiled avuncularly. "Well, apparently one of the major studios wants to do a "reality" series about high school, about the pressures, the joys, the difficulties of being a teenager…and they want you to star in it."

Yuriko looked thoughtful. "Am I playing a boy or a girl?"

"You're not playing anyone." Miyamoto put his hand on her shoulder. "You're playing yourself."

"What?"

"We've enrolled you in Mitsukawa High School as a senior. Just be yourself. The film crew will try to stay out of your way as much as possible, remain in the background. We've already made arrangements with the administration. You have nothing to worry about," Miyamoto reassured her. With a comforting pat, he removed his hand from her shoulder.

"Just remember to do your homework!" Laughing at his joke, he turned away from the stunned blonde and headed towards the office door. "Kishi-san, if you have any questions, give me a call." Kishi bowed as he finished, and didn't straighten up until Miyamoto had left the office.

The manager gave her client a nasty grin. "Sounds like fun, doesn't it?"

Yuriko made a face. "Oh, great. Because high school was so much fun the *first* time around…"

***

Back to School

Yuriko lifted one hanger to her chin, then the other. She tried to imagine each outfit on her body, but the images just didn't work. She looked at Mariko in the mirror, pretending not to see the evil grin her friend was giving her.

"Which one do you think I should wear on my first day?" Yuriko asked, switching hangers once again. "Boy's or girl's?"

Mariko put a hand to her chin thoughtfully. "Try them on, let's see what they look like."

Yuriko shot her friend a suspicious look and entered the dressing room. When she came out, she was wearing the girl's uniform. Yuriko clasped her hands in front of her waist and waited for Mariko's verdict.

Mariko looked her up and down and nodded. "You know, you look better in that than I would have suspected." She grimaced. "I forgot that about you…you always make your clothes look good."

Yuriko smirked a bit and pulled gently at the hem of her skirt, lifting it slightly. "You don't think my legs will be too distracting?"

Mariko stuck her tongue out. "Probably. Let's see the boy's now." She shooed Yuriko back into the dressing room. When the blonde came out a second time, Mariko gave a low whistle. "Don't do that, it's bad for my heart!" she laughed. The stiff, military-style uniform looked splendid on Yuriko, and Mariko could tell that her friend knew it.

"There is something to be said for custom tailoring," Yuriko commented, turning to the mirror and smoothing the jacket across her hips.

"Okay." Mariko rendered the verdict at last. "I'm saying start with boy's, but wear the girl's the second day, so they don't get any chances to make assumptions."

"What?" Yuriko asked with a grin. "Like that I might be a crossdressing lesbian or something?" She laughed. "Wouldn't want them to get any funny ideas like that."

Mariko protested, "No, I didn't mean that…okay, yes I did. Forget it. Wear the boy's." She smiled at Yuriko admiring herself in the mirror. "You always were a little vain."

"Mari, thank you." Yuriko took both her friend's hands in her own and looked down at the brunette fondly.

"Whatever for?" Mariko looked puzzled.

"For saying *exactly* what you're thinking." Yuriko leaned down and bussed Mariko on the cheek. "I'm going to need you more, while I do this stupid project."

Mariko blushed prettily. "I've been your friend a long time, Yuri. I don't plan on going away anytime soon."

***

The nightmare starts early, Yuriko thought. She was pretty much a morning person these days, since most shoots began earlier than people thought. Getting ready for school wasn't that much of an issue. She smiled brightly as she combed her hair, thinking of how her old homeroom teacher would have laughed to see her now. She had so many "tardy"s on her school record it almost wasn't funny.

Book bag in hand, uniform neatly pressed, Yuriko had the car let her off about a block away from school. She walked along with the other students, none of whom appeared to know her - or even notice a new student walking with them at all. She relaxed slightly, and was surprised to note that she was actually rather tense to begin with.

It was just after entering the main gate that it started. She was walking briskly towards the school entrance when a harsh voice rang out.

"Hey! Hey you!"

She slowed her steps slightly.

"Yo, pretty boy! Yeah, you!" A second voice laughed cruelly.

Yuriko turned to see four disheveled figures slouching along the brick wall. She pointed at herself and asked, "Are you talking to me?"

The first voice belonged to a stocky young man whose upper lip was in need of a shave. His uniform jacket was unfastened and there were worn areas at the wrist and elbows. "Yeah, I'm talkin' to you. You see anyone else here?"

Yuriko did, in fact. At least thirty students were now slowing their progress, watching the interaction.

"No." She smiled. "No one else at all."

The ringleader pushed himself off the wall and approached her belligerently. She found herself staring him nearly in the eyes. He leaned forward and growled, "What are you - some kind of fag?"

She thought about that for a split second, batted her eyelashes at him and preened. "No," she said, softening her voice and raising its pitch slightly, "I'm a girl."

Yuri could hear the snickers come from the students around her. She wanted to glance over her shoulder and see if the camera crew had arrived yet, but remembered she was to meet them in the Principal's office. She groaned inwardly.

The ringleader turned red and spluttered, "I guess we're going to have to teach you a lesson so we get some respect."

Yuriko yawned delicately and looked at her watch. She patted the ringleader lightly on the arm and said, "You can beat me silly, but to be honest, you'll never get an ounce of respect out of me. Now if you'll excuse me..." she turned away to the sound of thirty gasps of surprise.

Welcome to your first day of high school, Yuri, she thought wryly.

***

"Welcome to your first day of high school!" The principal looked like every principal since the dawn of time. His beaming smile masked his intense dislike for youth and his fear of rebellion. Yuriko bowed deeply and thanked him for allowing her to be a part of his school, yadda, yadda, yadda.... He welcomed her fulsomely, and introduced her to her homeroom teacher. Yuriko turned towards the young man and bowed. When she stood upright once again, she glanced at him in some surprise.

Abe-sensei was young, probably not much older than she was. What was more, she thought as she eyed him critically, *I'd bet ten thousand yen that he's...*, her thoughts were interrupted by the arrival of the camera crew.

The arrangements were simple. A single cameraman would discreetly film her classes, while the full crew would be available for interviews with her, and outside activities. Yuriko rolled her eyes as she realized that the only time she'd have to herself would be in the bathroom...she hoped.

Eventually the formalities ended. It was close to the end of homeroom, so Abe-sensei suggested that he and Yuriko make the best of their time. The two left the principal's office with many a bow, followed by a cameraman and a production assistant who looked exhausted already.

Abe-sensei looked behind him nervously. Whispering to Yuriko, he asked, "Is that woman going to be alright? She looks terrible."

Yuriko smiled reassuringly. "She's a PA - they all look like that." Abe-sensei nod-

Name: Hayashi Mariko

Birthday: September 18

Zodiac Sign: Virgo

Blood Type: B

Occupation: Assistant Producer of TV Game Shows

Favorite Color: Emerald Green

Favorite Food: Kabocha, Gratin

Favorite Music: Top 40

Least Favorite Things: Snobby People, Sewing

ded, but did not look happy, or enlightened.

They reached the room and slid the door open. Abe-sensei entered and the students stood; then, at his nod, were seated. "Everyone, I'd like to introduce you to a new student. She'll be with us for a while..." He looked down at the folder he held in his hand. "Please make, uh, Yuriko, welcome..." His voice was drowned out by the buzz of voices in the classroom as Yuriko stepped in.

She bowed and smiled. "My name is Yuriko. Nice to meet you." The buzz continued and she stood, content to wait it out.

Abe-sensei looked completely flustered until one girl, her hand raised, stood shyly and asked, "Excuse me. Are you *the* Yuriko?"

Yuriko nodded and said, "I guess my reputation precedes me, huh?" Abe-sensei looked from the girl to Yuriko and back. "*The* Yuriko?" He asked, puzzled.

The girl shot him a disdainful glance, then turned back to Yuriko with hearts in her eyes. "Are you really filming a new show here?"

Yuri gestured to the cameraman in the corner. "Apparently." To which answer, the girls in the class practically shrieked with delight, while the boys all muttered and wondered amongst themselves.

Abe-sensei attempted to regain order, but one of the boys stood up and asked loudly, "Is it true what they say, did you really face down Uto and his gang this morning?" Silence fell and Yuriko grimaced internally. Yep, just the normal life of a high school student.

"Um, not really." The buzz was disappointed.

Abe-sensei used the lull to assign Yuriko a seat. She placed her bag on the desk and bowed briefly to the girl in the next seat. The girl giggled and turned red from her neck to her ears. It took everything Yuriko had not to place her face in her hands and whimper.

Volume 1, Issue 3

New Student Blues

Physical education! How *had* she forgotten about that? Yuriko tried not to openly grimace as she entered the locker room with the other girls. It wasn't that she was a prude...it's just that these girls were girls...little girls. Yucko. Yuriko kept her eyes frozen on her locker or her clothes as she changed, pretending not to notice the shy glances, the blushes, the whispers. She longed for a drink, preferably something strong and mind-numbing. How the hell had she gotten through this the first time around, she wondered. Oh, yeah, she smiled to herself, I remember now...Junko. Man, was she beautiful. Yuriko smiled brightly now and joined the rest of the girls in the gym, her mind filled with memories of her first love.

"Today we're playing basketball," the coach said. Yuriko couldn't remember her name yet. Ma - something. "Are you okay with that?" Yuriko's head shot up suddenly, when she realized she was being spoken to.

"Uh, yeah, sure...I'm not great at it, though." Yuriko grinned; two girls to her right sighed breathily. Yuriko remonstrated with herself. Great - gotta watch that.

The next few minutes were odd...teams were drawn up, and positions assigned. Because of her height, Yuriko was naturally assigned to center. *There's no time like the present to make a fool of myself*, she thought, and took the ball as it was passed to her. To her surprise, a spin and several steps later, she was leaping to make a shot...and the ball went in.

"I thought you said you weren't good at this game," the coach said teasingly.

Yuriko laughed. "Well, I wasn't, last time I played. About five years ago."

The coach gave her an appraising look. "Stop by my office after school. We could use you on the basketball team." Yuriko bowed slightly, then mentally slapped herself. *What the hell are you *doing* Yuri? Team sports? Where's the little intellectual I know and love?*

"Uh, Sensei?" Yuriko asked, as the coach turned back to the game. "Does this school have a poetry club?" The sound of more sighs. Ugh.

The coach shook her head. "But we have a writing club, maybe you can ask them."

Yuriko nodded in thanks. She sat on the bench and turned to the two girls next to her. "Hi - I'm Yuriko." They stared at her in shock for a full second, then burst out giggling. With an intense effort of will, she did *not* roll her eyes. In the middle of the giggles she was able to make out two names, Emi and Sumika.

***

The end of the school day could not come fast enough. Yuriko was shocked at how much science she remembered, how much math she had forgotten, and how very, very bad her language skills were. She looked forlornly at the pile of homework on her desk. This sucked.

While she packed her bag, the girl next to her stood to leave. Yuriko stopped her and apologized. "Sayaka-san, right?" Sayaka blushed, but thankfully, did not giggle. "Do you know where the Writing Club meets? I want to talk to them about joining."

Sayaka's coloring rose. "I'm..." she hesitated, then lowered her eyes. "I'm the president of that club. You can come with me - we'd like it very much if you joined." She bowed, and kept her eyes on the floor.

Yuriko stepped away from her desk and stood in front of the girl. Lifting

Sayaka's chin with her finger, Yuriko looked down into the girl's eyes.

"Thanks. But, if I'm going to join, we have to make a deal here." Yuriko put one hand on her hip. "None of this blushing stuff. I'm just another student, okay?"

Sayaka bowed again, and turned quickly, practically running to the door. "You can follow me, Yuriko-sam-...Yuriko-san," she said, softly.

"-kun." Yuriko said, following her out into the hallway. "I'll need a sempai around here to show me the ropes. Are you busy later?" Sayaka stared at her with huge eyes. Yuriko looked at her questioningly. "What? Do I have something on my face?" She reached up to brush her cheek but Sayaka began to laugh.

"No, nothing on your face. You're just so...different."

Yuriko grinned. "Forward? Impudent? Rude?"

"Yes," Sayaka confirmed, "all those things. And adult too. You're not a high school student and it shows. You don't talk the same, or act the same."

They turned a corner and stopped in front of a classroom door. Yuriko put her hand on the door and smiled at Sayaka. "I never was much good at being like everyone else."

Sayaka smiled back. "No - I suppose that's why you're famous and we, the rest of us, the ones who are good at being the same, aren't."

Yuriko nodded at this. "That's pretty wise coming from a high school student." She slid the door open and gestured Sayaka to precede her.

***

Matsumori-sensei. That was it. Eventually, Yuriko would remember all the teachers' names. The coach met Yuriko at the door of her office and waved her in.

"You've created quite a stir in our school," Matsumori-sensei commented, gesturing her to a chair. She pulled her hair back into a ponytail, Yuriko noticed - it made her look more severe, and older, than she really was.

Yuriko sat and looked around. The coach had her own office, of a sort, rather than using the teacher's room. Yuriko could see equipment and trophies piled haphazardly together. She liked the woman immediately. Anyone who was this sloppy was probably okay.

"Yes, well, it wasn't really my idea," Yuriko explained. "My agent decided this would be good for me. I'm not really sure it's good for anyone."

The other woman nodded. "Until everyone gets used to your presence, I'd say it's going to be awkward. Feel free to drop by, if you need someone to talk to."

26

"Thanks." Yuriko said, sincerely. "I might need a few friends."

"If I remember your file correctly, we actually share a birthday," the coach said. "I was born in Hokkaido, though. You were born in Tokyo, correct?"

"Uh, yeah." Yuriko looked a little put out. "Sorry," she said a moment later. "It always annoyed me that teachers have all this information about students, but not the other way around."

The coach looked startled, then laughed. "How rude of me. Let's start again. I'm Matsumori Ruriko. I coach girls' basketball, teach PE and make a great strawberry shortcake." She extended a hand and Yuriko took it. Her shake was strong.

"Yuriko, no family name, I can't cook to save my soul, but I'm told that I'm not bad looking and can act a little." Yuriko scratched her head. "Not really much of a recommendation, is it?"

Matsumori-sensei laughed again. "Nope, but don't tell the girls here, they'll scratch your eyes out."

"Oh, that," Yuriko sighed.

Something sparkled in the coach's eye as she leaned forward and asked, "Are you as much the playboy, er, girl, as the press makes you out to be?"

"Um, probably not." Yuriko evaded the question, but the coach didn't let it pass.

"C'mon...between friends..." there was something conspiratorial in Matsumori-sensei's smile and Yuriko nodded. She turned to the camera-man behind her and shot him a questioning glance. He pulled the camera off his shoulder and nodded. "I'll be outside having a cigarette." He turned and practically shoved the PA out of the office with him.

When the door closed behind them, Yuriko nodded again at the coach.

"But," she insisted, "I'm not interested in teenyboppers. So there won't be any problems with..."

The coach waved away her concerns. "I'll vouch for you. You don't seem predatory."

Yuriko smiled, evilly. "I can be..."

Matsumori-sensei returned the grin. "So can I, if he's worth the effort." She caught the other woman's eye and they laughed.

***

Home Stretch

Yuriko yawned luxuriously. Finally, she could go home. She glanced at her watch, 5:30. Her stomach rumbled and she smiled down at it. "Soon, soon." She knew the car would be waiting for her outside and every bone in her exhausted body longed to relax into its plush interior.

She turned to the cameraman who stood off to her right and waved. "Night."

He waved back from behind the camera. Yuriko could hear the PA wish her a good evening distractedly, as she talked to the other cameraman about editing today's footage. Yawning again, she started for the street.

The shove didn't knock her off her feet, but it did push her back a few steps. She stared in surprise as Uto and his henchmen faced off between her and her waiting car. She smiled condescendingly.

"Look boys..."

Uto interrupted. "Shut your trap, you dyke."

Yuriko's eyebrow rose at that. She noticed two of the toughs trying to out-flank her, so she backed herself up to the brick wall that led to the school. "Jealous already?" she taunted lightly. "I haven't even seduced your girl-friends yet."

Uto's teeth ground audibly. "You think you're pretty clever, don't you?" He laughed nastily. "You think you don't have to be afraid of us."

Yuriko shook her head. "That's ridiculous. I'm terrified of you. I have every confidence in your ability to beat me to dirt. But what does that have to do with the way I dress or who I sleep with?"

This appeared to stun Uto into momentary silence. He stood, his fists clenched, sneering at Yuriko.

She saw the cameraman move closer, the tape still rolling. Great, thanks for the backup.... She looked Uto in the eye and wasn't sure she liked what she saw. Uto glared at her a moment more, then asked, intensely, "Are you making fun of me?"

Yuriko was startled by this question. "Uh, no...why would I do that? Look," she replied earnestly, gesturing at the four boys. "You are, collectively, several hundred kilograms heavier than me. I'm sure you're all strong and tough and good fighters. I'm not. If you beat me up, I won't be any more afraid of you than I am already. You'd have a Pyrrhic victory. And the police would have a tape of you beating the shit out of me, so when I pressed charges, you'd have no way to deny it." She pointed to the cameraman. Uto turned and gazed over his shoulder for a moment, then turned back.

"We could always wait until you were alone," Uto threatened.

Yuriko threw up her hands in disgust. "Fine! Fine. Do it. Beat me up already. Sheesh. Do you think for a moment that I'd hesitate to use my notoriety to have your asses sent to prison? Remember, the whole world will see you threaten me on VIDEO." She stood, trying not to shake with tension. Her stomach felt sour.

She heard Uto laugh shortly, then again. The next thing she knew Uto was laughing quite raucously, and eventually the three henchmen joined him. It was quite a laughfest, she thought, as a nervous grin broke out on her own face.

Uto stopped laughing for a moment and peered at her strangely. She realized that he had weak eyes. Odd thing for a gang leader, she thought.

"You're one strange chick," he said approvingly.

"Uh, yeah," Yuriko said. "Thanks, I guess."

Uto gestured to himself, then each of the other guys in turn. "I'm Uto, this is Heiji," he gestured at a surfer boy next to him, "Ni-ru," a boy with a pierced ear and a tooth missing nodded at her, "and this is Togai, my brother."

Brother? Togai stood tall and lanky, while Uto was short and stocky. They looked as different as night and day.

"Uh, hi," Yuriko said, wishing to hell she was home. "Yuriko."

"Yuri-chan," Uto said condescendingly, "don't go near our girlfriends, or we'll beat the living shit out of you."

"Right. I promise." Yuriko spotted the car and edged her way towards it. With a few last words, she parted from the gang and, with an enormous sigh, let the car drive her away.

***

"My hero" Mariko said teasingly. She and Hachi sat on the sofa, while Yuriko had laid herself out supine on the floor.

"Don't," Yuriko pleaded. "I've had a terrible day," she groaned in misery. "And I have homework to do!" She glared as

Name: Kishi ?

Birthday: August 3

Zodiac Sign: Leo

Blood Type: AB

Occupation: Talent Manager

Favorite Color: Sky Blue

Favorite Food: Omelet

Favorite Music: Minami Haruo

Least Favorite Things: Arrogant Idols, Yogurt

Mariko and Hachi chuckled. "It's not funny! I have to write in English... an essay on how I spent my summer vacation."

Mariko snorted. "You can't do that, can you?"

Yuriko put her hands over her face. "Probably not. I doubt the teacher expects an essay on the joys of a Alpine chateau and a French actress." Yuriko sat up and grabbed her glass of wine, gulping it down in one go. "The worst part is the giggling, though," she commented off-handedly.

"Then maybe you *should* write up your essay..." Hachi suggested. "The giggling will be replaced by shocked silence." He pretended to flinch from the look Yuriko shot him.

"You two are worse than nothing! Out!" Yuriko stood, and began to herd them off the couch. "If you're not helping with my homework, then out!"

"Fine, fine!" Mariko took Hachi's arm and gathered up her coat as they headed towards the door. "But the next time you need help with algebra, don't come crying to me!" Her laughter could be heard, even after Yuriko slammed the door behind her.

Yuriko took one look at the book bag on the table and found herself sinking onto the sofa face first. "What I did on my summer vacation..."

Volume 1, Issue 5

I Enjoy Being a Girl

Yuriko swung her legs out of the car and lifted herself from the seat. She picked up her book bag, ran her hand down her thigh to smooth out wrinkles and thanked the driver. Shutting the car door, she headed for school.

She turned the corner and past the school gate, a happy bounce in her step despite the bags under her eyes. Yuriko wasn't the kind of woman to let too little sleep get her down. In fact, sometimes too little sleep was a good thing....

The first whistle went by unnoticed, because all the girls were so busy whispering "cu-u-ute." The second, followed by a harsh, "Hey, babe!" made her look up sharply. Her smile faded when she noticed Uto and his cronies leaning on the wall in their accustomed spot.

"Yo, Yuri-chan!" Uto waved facetiously. "Nice gams."

Yuriko looked down at her legs, and back at the boys. She gave them an impudent grin.

Heiji whistled again and said, "Hey, dolly, wanna do me?"

Yuriko tossed her hair out of her eyes and began walking towards the school. Smiling over her shoulder, she blew them a kiss. "You wish, surfer boy."

There was a moment of silence, then loud laughing broke out behind her. A voice called out, "Hey, Yuri-chan…?"

She stopped and looked back again. Togai was standing away from the

wall, looking as polite as he could. "Yes?" she asked mildly.

He shuffled his feet a moment or two and asked in a rush, "What's Pyrrhic mean?"

Yuriko laughed and turned away. "Look it up To-kun. Girls love smart guys."

"Yeah?"

Yuriko's laugh was louder than strictly necessary. She ignored both staring boys and whining girls and entered school.

***

Sayaka smiled at Yuriko as the blonde seated herself. Along with the regulation dress for girls, Yuriko had decided to wear earrings, just as a way of playing the gender mind-fuck for all it was worth. She might even get her nails painted next week - that would look great with the boy's uniform, Yuriko laughed to herself. After all, accessorizing was everything.

Turning to Sayaka, Yuriko inquired how the girl was. Trying her best not to blush, Sayaka said that she was well.

"How are you today, Yuriko-…" the girl hesitated at the honorific, then grinned up at Yuriko, "-chan, today, I suppose?" She laughed at Yuriko's expression.

"Is it really that big a thing?" Yuriko looked down at the skirt she wore.

Sayaka shook her head. "I was only teasing…"

Yuriko looked startled, then smiled. "Whatever you say, sempai."

Now it was Sayaka's turn to look startled. The two women laughed together for a while, until they were called to stand for the teacher.

Abe-sensei looked slightly more rumpled that he had the day before. Yuriko guessed that it was habitual look. Poor guy probably went through life slightly bewildered all the time. She stifled a yawn and waited for him to take attendance.

"Yuriko?" His voice was raised slightly. He looked up, sliding his eyes past Yuriko's face. "Yuriko?"

"Here!" Yuriko called out briskly. She made a little prediction about what would happen, then grinned when everyone acted predictably. First, the teacher looked at her, frowning. She pushed the long hair back from her right temple and smiled at him.. He looked startled at the appearance of a strange girl in Yuriko's seat. Realization set in at the same time the general buzz cottoned to the fact that Yuriko was in girl's uniform today. The teacher's eyes tightened slightly, but he turned back to his attendance sheet and duly made a mark.

Yuriko heard a low whistle, and laughed at the boys trying to get a look at her legs without looking like they were looking. How silly they all were. When homeroom was over, she guessed that she had never seen the boys stand *quite* so quickly before. Sayaka caught her eye and they grinned at each other.

Abe-sensei might have been a little cold, but he was nothing compared to Sawako-sensei, her math teacher. Later, Yuriko confided to Sayaka that her math teacher in high school the first time around had been a bastard, too.

Sawako-sensei made a habit of pinching his lips together, as if he smelled something bad in the room. His piggy little eyes followed her unpleasantly when she stood to do a problem on the board…and he seemed to call on her a lot.

"I can't stand algebra." Yuriko said, when at last they were free of the class. Sayaka nodded understandingly.

"There's a rumor," Sayaka said, a bit hesitantly, "that Sawako-sensei is abusive to students in other ways as well."

Yuriko's eyebrow rose. "Indeed?" She thought that sometimes having a camera crew tagging along for your life wasn't *such* a bad thing. "Like, abuse-abuse, or emotional abuse?"

Sayaka shook her head. "I don't know…it's just rumors. But there was an incident last year." She looked around carefully and lowered her voice. "A girl had to stay late and do extra work for him…she was rushed to the hospital and he was suspended for a week."

"Did he hit her or…" Yuriko felt something ominous and threatening on the edge of this conversation.

"We don't know. She never came back to school." Sayaka gestured down a hall. "Shall we eat outside today? It's so beautiful."

Yuriko relaxed her face, which had become tense. "Sure!" She automatically sprang forward to get the door for Sayaka, and bowed slightly as she let the younger woman through. Sayaka laughed at her and Yuriko stood, coloring slightly.

"Sorry. I forget that today I can leave the chivalry behind." Yuriko's voice was self-deprecating.

"So, you're not as complacent about what you wear as you seem, then?" Sayaka asked, then immediately apologized.

The two women sat down at a table outside. Yuriko found herself practically wolfing her lunch. The cameraman and PA had wandered off to have their own meals and Yuriko found herself alone with her new "sempai."

"It's a little more complicated than that," Yuriko said. "Back when I *was* in school, I guess I didn't care much, but then, I had no idea who I was anyway. After I realized that I liked looking good - and that I look as good in a tie as a skirt, so I just got used to it. Well, that's the simple version, anyway."

Sayaka looked down into her bentou box thoughtfully. "Please don't answer this if I'm being rude, but…" she paused while she phrased her sentence carefully, "Why don't you use a family name? Why just 'Yuriko'?"

Yuriko started to put her hands behind her head, then thought twice about it, when her blouse began to ride up over her midriff. She settled for leaning back. Looking at the girl across from her, Yuriko gave her a wry grin.

"What's with the interview - you get a job with the production company or something?"

Sayaka's eyes widened, and she had the sense to look abashed. "No! It's not that…" her face changed and she leaned forward, asking eagerly, "But that's such a great idea! Would you mind that? Doing an interview for the writing club?

"Yeah, I guess that would be okay." Yuriko couldn't see any problem with that.

"So?" Sayaka insisted. Yuriko raised an eyebrow.

"Do you want the goofy answer or the serious one?"

Sayaka considered. "Both. Goofy first."

"Goofy first. Well, hey - it works for Madonna!" Her voice took on a 'television' cadence and Sayaka giggled. "Serious? Well, let's just say that I don't have a family anymore."

"Are they all gone?" Sayaka asked sadly.

"Gone? No. More like I'm the one that's gone."

"Oh," Sayaka said.

"Pretty much." Yuriko finished the last bites of her lunch and closed the box up.

"But…didn't they try and contact you when you became famous?"

Yuriko waggled her eyebrows comically. "Infamous, you mean. And no. To be honest, I think it's better for all of us this way." The bell rang, announcing the end of lunchtime and Yuriko stood.

"Shall we?" She gestured back towards the school. "Once more into the breach," she commented in English.

"Oh, that's good!" Sayaka said, approvingly. "You ought to use that in class!"

Laughing, they walked back into the school building.

Volume 1, Issue 6

Love and Hate on the Court

One of the nice things about school, Yuriko thought as she walked towards the lockers, was the end of the day. It was like you'd actually accomplished something, having made it through one more day filled with random commands and strange requests (if you looked at them from a bigger perspective).... She stopped in her tracks.

Approaching her locker slowly, she could make out what appeared to be an envelope sticking out from one of the ventilation slits. How odd.

She pulled at the envelope and was not terribly surprised to find that it was a love letter. She wondered why the sender hadn't shoved it all the way through the slot, and smiled when she guessed it was due to extreme nervousness. That was understandable, after all. She lifted the note to her nose and gently sniffed. There was no scent. Probably a boy's then. Smiling, she tucked it under her arm and lifted the locker door.

Her smile faded as tens, no, dozens of little envelopes in every size, shape and color, cascaded out of her shoe locker, past her flailing hands and landed in scattered piles on the floor around her feet. She stared down in disbelief at the paper that now littered the floor, while a few stragglers slithered their way out of the locker to join their brethren. Looking up, Yuriko heard a noise to her left and she turned to see today's cameraman moving in for a close-up. She gave a wan smile and waved, then let the locker door drop, and softly banged her forehead against it.

***

When Yuriko at last entered the gym, she found it already crowded with girls in uniform. Squeaking from sneakers on waxed floors, shouts and the coach calling out commands filled the air. Girls' voices cheered, cajoled and shrieked at each turn of the game in progress. Yuriko was content to stand in the back and watch the action.

It was almost immediately apparent that the powerhouse of the team was a long-limbed girl, whose long black hair was pulled into a tight ponytail. Her presence on the court was electrifying. She moved with a grace that was unusual for a teenager...and her commands to her team radiated assurance. Yuriko nodded approvingly. This would be the team captain.

Matsumori-sensei blew her whistle and called a short break. Both sides turned towards the benches, grabbing for waterbottles and towels. The coach waved the dark-haired girl over and started towards Yuriko.

The girl's ponytail bounced behind her as she jogged over. "Yes, Coach?" Her voice was clipped, precise.

Matsumori-sensei gestured towards the blonde and made introductions. Yuriko offered her hand and bowed, stated her name and class and watched for the reaction. The girl's nostrils flared slightly at her name, but no other change came over her face.

"I'm Kaori. Yamamoto Kaori. Nice to meet you." The clipped voice was ambiguous - Yuriko couldn't be sure whether the girl was pleased or not.

The coach was already speaking. "She's here for a while and I thought, with her height, she'd be a good addition to the team. I'd like you to watch her play, and we can talk about where she might be useful."

"Uh," Yuriko interrupted, "I can't play in games, you know that, right? I'm not technically eligible." She shrugged. "But I'll be glad to help out in practice." She could see Kaori watching her closely and felt oddly uncomfortable under the girl's stare.

"Let's take it one step at a time, shall we?" Matsumori-sensei asked. "You feel up to a little one on one?" She handed a ball to Yuriko, who nodded, a little unsure of herself.

Smiling at Kaori, she said, "I'm not all that good..."

Kaori turned away as she spoke, "I'll be the judge of that."

Yuriko's eyebrows lifted, then lowered. Ni-i-ce.... She headed onto the floor, bouncing the ball lightly, getting a feel for it.

Kaori stood, her body ready, uncommitted. Yuriko passed the ball to her, and Kaori shot it back, hard. Yuriko received the ball and broke around to the right; Kaori was there in an instant, covering her, blocking her way to the basket. Yuriko tried to fake a shot, but Kaori read her intentions and almost took the ball away. Yuriko broke again and, after a few steps, crashed shoulder to chest with Kaori. The girl didn't flinch, but proceeded to get right in Yuriko's face. The blonde set her jaw and decided to let the slight height difference work. She leapt and shot, her hands just above the limit of Kaori's reach...but the ball rebounded from the hoop, and Kaori was there to take it.

The next few minutes were the toughest workout of Yuriko's life. Kaori had great intuition, good skill and was, Yuri was annoyed to note, in much better shape than herself. When the coach at last blew the whistle, Yuriko practically sank into the floor with relief and exhaustion. Kaori took one more leisurely shot, sank the basket and turned away without a word. Yuriko accepted a towel gratefully from one girl and a water bottle from another, but never took her eyes off the team captain.

The coach was at her elbow, grinning. "Not bad for your first day."

Yuriko returned the grin. "Not good, either. I'm out of shape - the celebrity life has made me soft." She gestured with her chin towards Kaori, who stood in the center of a ring of girls, talking with one or two of them. "She doesn't like me."

Shaking her head, Matsumori-sensei said, "Not much. Thinks you're a distraction. But I think you've got real potential." She looked over at her star forward. "She'll come around when she sees that you're sincere."

Yuriko flushed and lowered her voice. "But…she's right. I'm only doing this because I have to." Seeing the disappointed look on the coach's face, she backtracked. "I mean, I'll do my best, but I won't be here for long."

Matsumori-sensei looked thoughtful. "I'll talk to Kaori-kun..."

Yuriko interrupted. "No - I'll take care of it myself." She smiled reassuringly. "I'm good at that kind of thing."

The coach looked at Yuriko with a worried expression, then her face softened. "Okay, but if you need me to, I will." She turned back to the girls and separated them into two drill squads.

Yuriko found herself on a squad with ten teammates. She turned her mind to trying to keep up with the other girls, but had the constant, irritating sensation that she was being watched. At last she broke from her formation and shot a look towards the other side of the gym. There stood Kaori, her eyes burning darkly, staring directly at Yuriko. The team cap-

Name: Kawada Hachigoro

Birthday: May 6

Zodiac Sign: Taurus

Blood Type: B

Occupation: Account Manager

Favorite Color: Yellow

Favorite Food: Pasta

Favorite Music: Enka, esp. Sakamoto Fuyumi

Least Favorite Thing: Rainy Season

43

tain caught her eye then, slowly and deliberately, turned away.

Yuriko sighed, but her attention was drawn away again by one of the girls, who was explaining the next drill.

The afternoon passed slowly.

***

"Why are you torturing yourself?" Mari's voice was, over the phone, even gigglier than usual. Yuriko made a face at the phone tucked between shoulder and cheek. "You have an agency for that kind of thing."

"Because these kids took time to write me these notes..."

"Love letters," Mari interrupted, smirking audibly.

"Yes, love letters," Yuriko snapped. "And I feel like I should at least *read* them."

"What are you going to do about them? You can't very well respond to them all. You don't even know who half these people are."

Yuriko slit another one open and pulled out the neatly folded note. She read out loud, "'Yuriko-sama, I think you are the most wonderful singer and very beautiful in the girl's uniform. I love you very much.' No signature."

Mari's laughter was loud and Yuriko took the moment to lay the letter in the "unsigned" pile. The next one was obviously from a boy. The paper was dark, but had a small embossed English "R" in one corner. She read again, "'Yuriko-san, I'm sure you will receive many letters from many students, but I hope that mine is special. I have never heard you sing, although other students tell me that you are good. I haven't seen any of your acting, either. I am sorry about that, because I think you are very good-looking.'" Yuriko ignored the acerbic comment that came from the phone. "'I wanted to write you and say that I am glad you have come to our school and I hope that one day we will meet and be friends. Yours, Ryo.'"

"Well, that was different at least," Mari said, her voice faint.

"Stop doing that." Yuriko commented.

"What?" Mariko said, her voice clear once again.

"Kissing Hachi when you're on the phone. You can get off any time, you know." Yuriko opened another letter, scanned it and set it on the "signed with initials" pile.

"Oh, you!" Mariko said accusingly, then laughed. "And so I shall. Will we see you Saturday night?"

"Eight o'clock at Chuugoku." Yuriko stuck another unsigned note on the appropriate pile.

"See you then!" Mariko said and hung up the phone.

"I can't wait." Yuriko spoke to the dead air. "You have no idea." She took the phone from under her chin and closed it up, then slit open another letter.

***

Volume 1, Issue 7

Rhythm

"Good morning, Yuriko-kun!" Sayaka sounded extremely chipper.

"Good morning, sempai." Yuriko bowed to her "senior" and seated herself at her desk. Back in the boy's uniform, she realized she had forgotten to lose the earrings...oh well. She stifled a yawn, but the next one got through. The third was excessive, she thought, and she willed herself to not yawn again. She yawned again.

"Late night last night?" Sayaka inquired - rather archly, Yuriko noted.

"Yes, as a matter of fact. I was having difficulty with my Japanese homework." Yuriko shot the girl a self-righteous look. "I've forgotten a lot - and it doesn't reassure me to know that I can forget it all over again when I leave here. I'm not going to do well on today's test."

"Maybe you need a tutor." The voice came from behind Yuriko and she turned, rather more abruptly than she meant to. She stared at the mousy girl behind her and strained to remember her name.

"You're...uh..." Yuriko desperately wracked her memory, "Aya-san, right?"

A pleased smiled broke out across the girl's face. "That's right. I'm surprised you remembered." She looked Yuriko in the eye and said, "I'm not very memorable."

Yuriko couldn't really argue with that, but she did anyway. Aya seemed good-natured enough about it, though, and Yuriko took an instant liking to the girl.

"I'm sorry, we haven't really spoken since I got here," Yuriko said smoothly. "But I think your idea sounds like a good one. Do you know someone who can tutor me?"

Aya tightened her lips in thought. "I think I do. You're joining the writing club, right?"

Yuriko nodded.

"Hmmm…that's twice a week, and basketball is three times a week…you'll be hard pressed, unless…" Aya cocked her head and eyed Yuriko. "If you're really serious, I can tutor you on Saturdays. That's a good day for me, and none of the other clubs meet then."

"You tutor me?" Yuriko played mental catch-up.

Sayaka explained. "Aya-san is the best tutor in school. She tutors several of the younger students and a few of the older ones, as well. She's even the head of the advanced studies program in Japanese here."

Yuriko reappraised the mousy girl. "Well, then, I'd be honored." They agreed to meet in homeroom after classes were done on Saturday.

Well, Yuriko thought, pleased with herself, that solves that. A second later she groaned, realizing that she now had next to no personal time left to herself. *School is killing me*, she thought.

***

"Yuriko…san," Sawako-sensei barked out her name, but with an unpleasant slur on the honorific, as if she wasn't worthy of it. "Please come up to the board and answer the fifth problem."

Yuriko swallowed a sharp retort and stood at the board for a moment, before outlining the answer. Algebra wasn't her best subject, that was for sure.

"That is incorrect," Sawako-sensei snapped. "Sit down. Can anyone give me the *correct* answer?"

His insinuating tone was really getting on her nerves. She sighed and took her seat once again. A few classmates flashed sympathetic looks, but didn't dare turn their attention from the teacher for more than a moment. Yuriko rubbed her neck, trying to drain some of the tension from it.

***

"Man, he really has it out for you," one of the boys commented after class let out. "I've never seen him target someone like that."

Yuriko waved his concern away. "I seem to do that to people," she said, shoving nearly half a sandwich in her mouth at once. "Can't figure out why," she said around the food. The boy - Shiro, she thought - grinned and filled his own mouth with food. Today, three of the boys in class had asked to sit with her and Sayaka. Shiro seemed the most talkative of the three, the other two content to simply bask in his reflected glow.

Yuriko caught sight of Aya, and waved her over. Aya took a long look at the table and came over, hesitating slightly. One of the boys caught sight of her and looked away quickly, but when Yuriko caught his eyes, he pretended nothing was the matter.

"So," Shiro continued, "ole fish-face is going to try and break you, huh?" He grinned with relish. "Are you going to confront him on camera? Wouldn't that be something!"

"Hate to disappoint you," Yuriko commented placidly, "but I'm not going t confront him - on camera or off. He's allowed to not like me."

Shiro deflated. "Oh, well, yeah, I guess so," he said with considerable disappointment.

"Yuriko-kun," Sayaka interrupted, "I have something I need to do - I will see you at the writing club meeting today, right?" Yuriko shot her a look of thanks, and assured her that she would. Sayaka stood and took her leave.

Just as Shiro was gearing up for more gossip, Yuriko caught sight of the PA coming towards her, waving. Yuriko stood quickly. "Something's come up - must dash. Bye!" She made a hasty departure and intercepted the PA.

"Yuriko-san," the harried young woman said, "I have a message from Miyamoto-buchou. He says that he's scheduled an interview for you tomorrow, but that it has to be during the day." She pushed the hair out of her eyes with a limp hand. *Type 2' PA*, Yuriko commented to herself. "You'll have to leave class for it."

Yuriko nodded. Across the way, she could see the table she had vacated. Aya was eating her lunch, concentrating on her tray, while Shiro rattled on to one of the other boys. The third boy stared off into the distance, very obviously avoiding glancing at Aya.

"So, just remember," the PA continued, "I'll come and get you out of class."

"Sure, sure." Yuriko watched the third boy stand abruptly and walk away, while in her place Aya shrank into herself a little. Shiro talked on, unheeding. As did the PA. Yuriko reassured her that she understood the simple instructions, all the while watching Aya. At last, finished with her lunch, Aya gathered up her things, and left the grounds, heading in the opposite direction from the boy.

When the PA left, Yuriko stood and looked off in the direction that Aya had gone for a long while.

***

"Welcome to the writing club!" fifteen voices chorused happily. Yuriko bowed and greeted each one in turn. She seated herself at a desk, and watched the proceedings with interest.

Sayaka was a very competent leader, she noted with pleasure. She covered old business briskly, segued into new business neatly and had a crush the size of China on the vice-president. Yuriko smirked to herself. Every time the boy opened his mouth, poor Sayaka practically melted into a puddle right there. There was no doubt that he *was* a very pretty boy; his features were regular, clean-cut, his hair long and silky. He seemed perfect for her. She wondered why he didn't seem to notice.

Eventually Sayaka brought the meeting around to their new member. "Yuriko-kun has generously offered to do an interview with us for our journal - isn't that right?" The girl turned to the blonde, who straightened in her seat and answered with a sharp, "Yes, sempai!" then grinned as the club members laughed. Sayaka concluded the meeting at that, allowing each member to have a chance to talk to Yuriko.

The blonde was gracious and friendly, but she ached to leave. She watched Sayaka and the vice-president of the club move to the other side of the room for a few private words. Sayaka bowed, then turned to face Yuriko. Yuriko extricated herself from the crowd and joined her sempai at the door.

The vice president left the room and turned down the hallway. Yuriko watched Sayaka watching him, and said quietly, "Why don't you say something to him?"

Sayaka shook her head and clutched her books to her chest. "Watch."

Yuriko watched the tall boy move down the corridor. At the intersection of the halls, a girl came from around the corner and threw her arms around him. He smiled down at her happily and they walked off arm in arm.

"Ah," Yuriko commented.

"That's why," Sayaka said. She sighed, then pulled herself together, flashing a smile at her *kouhai*. "Tomorrow's Saturday! Then some fun."

The two women walked down the hall together, chatting about their plans for the weekend.

***

It Could Get Worse...

Some days just start bad and go downhill from there, Yuriko thought. She held her book bag over her head, but the rain dripped down her neck anyway. She sped her steps, then gave up all pretense of grace and began to run for the school, as the bell for homeroom rang.

Dripping, late, and looking very bedraggled, Yuriko made her way to her desk under the gimlet eye of Abe-sensei. He didn't say a word, but disapproval at her appearance was implicit.

At her desk, Yuriko pulled sodden hair away from her face and glanced at Sayaka, who gave her a quizzical look.

"Forgot an umbrella?" Sayaka whispered.

"Forgot I had to come to school on Saturday," Yuriko muttered. "I'm not used to six-day weeks."

Abe-sensei halted in midword to glare at Yuriko. She flashed him a repentant grin, and folded her hands neatly on the desk. He turned back to the announcements with a resigned air.

***

"Well," Yuriko commented to her friend between classes, "today couldn't get worse. I forgot to set my alarm, so I overslept. I was rushing out the door before I thought to check the weather. Great way to end my week!" Yuriko looked so unhappy that Sayaka giggled.

"At least you have tomorrow off."

"Hunh. With my luck, my agent has scheduled me on a kids show - or 'Stuntman for a Day'."

***

Sawako-sensei was as foul as the weather. He practically foamed at the mouth when Yuriko failed to complete the problem he assigned. Everyone in the class was tense as they waited for the real storm to blow in. It wasn't long in coming.

Thirty minutes into class the door slid open and the PA, looking more morose than usual, gestured for Yuriko to join her. Sawako-sensei glared at the young woman and demanded to know what she wanted.

The PA looked at Yuriko, frowning, then back at the burly teacher. "Uh, please forgive me, I was told you knew. Yuriko-san has an interview..."

Sawako-sensei closed the distance between them. His voice tight with anger, he said, "Get out."

The PA recoiled, but did not move, "Forgive me but..."

"I am trying to teach a class here. Get OUT!" He punctuated the last word by taking the door from the PA's hand and slamming it shut in front of her.

Yuriko found herself half out of her seat, when Sawako whirled on her. "You - sit," he commanded her. She sat. Sawako-sensei then rounded on the cameraman and pointed towards the door. "You too, get out. This is not a studio, this is a classroom!" He gestured angrily and the cameraman began to move towards the door - albeit slowly, and while the camera continued to roll.

Sawako-sensei saw to it that the door to the classroom was shut before he returned his attention to his students. Without missing a beat he snapped, "Yamada-kun, problem number thirteen please."

The class barely breathed. The tension was so thick no one dared make a sound, or move unecessarily. Sawako-sensei watched them all with a baleful eye, but his gaze most often lingered on Yuriko. She was sure she had two holes burnt in her forehead from his stare.

Time crawled. It was so silent in class that even the squeak of chalk made everyone jump. So, it practically stopped their hearts when there was a knock on the classroom door. It slid open smoothly and the school principal stepped into the room. Yuriko could see the PA standing behind him, her eyes red and angry.

The principal gestured for Sawako-sensei to come over and the math teacher did so, unwillingly. The principal's low rumble was audible, but no distinct words could be heard. When Sawako returned to his desk, he looked as if he had eaten something extremely bitter. The principal glanced at Yuriko and nodded. So relieved was she, that she literally bounded across the room, not caring that she looked as desperate as she felt.

After math, the interview was a welcome and pleasant interlude.

***

In fact, the interview had been awful. Distracted by the tension with her math teacher, Yuriko hadn't noticed that her head had become stuffed - she had a cold coming on, probably from her earlier drenching. The interviewer was more than a little hostile, and his piggy eyes had an unpleasant look in them, as he kept drawing the conversation away from her work and back to her reputation, and her sexuality. It seemed that the end would never come.

She ended the interview with a curt nod of thanks and watched with relief as the PA hustled the man and his crew away. She sighed, and then shivered as a chill moved up her spine.

"Well," she said hopefully to the cameraman, "at least it couldn't get much worse."

He lit a cigarette and nodded. "Sure it could."

Yuriko shot him a deadly look.

***

"A sixty-two?" Yuriko held the offending piece of paper as if it were a poisonous snake. "I can't believe it. That's terrible." She waved the test at Sayaka, who took it and looked it over.

"You're right, this *is* terrible," the girl announced.

"No, that's fine - just tell everyone why don't you," Yuriko mumbled. A sneeze rocked her body and she groaned.

"At least you'll have a tutor - you'll pass the next test," Sayaka reassured her.

"With a score like that, we'd better start today." Aya leaned forward to be heard. "Right after school."

The sound of steps made the three women turn, to see the class leader, Sato Hiroyuki, standing in front of them looking a little embarrassed.

"I'm very sorry to interrupt..." he began, obviously uncomfortable. Yuriko waved his concerns away and asked him to continue. "Uh, well, it has to do with day duty."

Yuriko watched as his face flushed. Cute kid. "Uh-huh..." she said encouragingly.

"Well, next week is your turn," he said quickly, not meeting her eyes.

"What?" she asked a little sharply. "How could that be? I just got here."

Hiroyuki bowed and stuttered an effuse apology. "I'm sorry, it's just that we're at the end of the alphabet and since you go by your given name..." he bowed again.

Yuriko laid her head on the desk and whined in self-pity.

***

Never had her apartment seemed so wonderful, so welcoming...so in need of a cleaning. Yuriko slouched in past the rumpled sofa, the ever-growing piles of love letters and unread scripts, past the unwashed dishes, and into the bedroom.

Falling face first on her bed, Yuriko moaned and groaned until all her self-pity welled up in a barrage of cursing. She cursed the weather, Sawako-sensei, her agent, the gods that apparently hated her and were punishing her for some terrible crime done in her past. When she was done cursing, she got up and muttered a few extra general imprecations for good measure. She stripped off her soaked uniform, threw it on a pile of unwashed laundry, which she otherwise ignored. Sliding the door to the bathroom open, she laid her glasses on the sink, and looked at herself in the mirror. Her normally bright - if weak - eyes were watery and her brow furrowed. She gave herself a wry smile and slid the cover off the *furo*.

The most wonderful thing about this apartment, she thought, as she slid in with a sigh of satisfaction, was the bathroom.

***

Yuriko slid the comb through her hair, set it down and straightened her tie. She checked the clock - she had plenty of time. The bath seemed to have knocked out the cold, thank heavens. She patted herself down, gave herself a wink in the mirror and smiled. *This* was more like it...playing school kid just wasn't really her style.

As she left her apartment she could hear

Name: Akaishi Sayaka

Birthday: June 2

Zodiac Sign: Gemini

Blood Type: A

Occupation: Honor Student, President of the Writing Club

Favorite Color: Pink

Favorite Food: Chocolate

Favorite Music: Top 40

Least Favorite Thing: The Dentist, Cooked Tomatoes

the phone ringing, but decided not to get it. The answering machine would
pick it up.

***

Saturday Night

"*Kampai!*" Yuriko drank her beer with relish. Being an adult had it all over being a kid.

Mari and Hachi joined her with their own toasts and the three settled themselves down for the long haul. This restaurant was a favorite with the studio crowd; Yuriko could see several faces she knew - a few of them, very well indeed. She caught a wink from one of the women across the room and raised her glass, then turned back to her friends.

"So," Hachi said, "I hear you've really made a splash at school in your first week."

Yuriko pushed her glasses back on her nose and leaned her elbows on the table. "I really don't want to talk about it, okay? Tonight I'm an adult again, I want to talk about things that are important...not essays and math problems." She sighed a little and ran her fingers through her hair.

Mari patted her lightly on the shoulder. "Poor Yuri. This has been a lot harder than you thought, hasn't it?" Yuri nodded, pouting, then smiled as Hachi poured her another glass. Her smile broadened as the waitress came over to take their order.

Hachi watched in amazement as Yuriko took over the conversation. In seconds the waitress was talking exclusively to her, laughing and flirting with the blonde as if they were old friends. He caught Mari's eye and they smiled at their friend's behavior.

When their orders had been placed by Yuriko - who had ordered for all of them - the waitress took her leave, with a last glance over her shoulder at the table. Yuriko's spirits seemed to have improved immensely by this point.

"I don't know how you do it," Hachi said, a little enviously. "that's a heck of a magic power you have."

Yuriko grinned. "I like to think of it as good interpersonal skills." They laughed. "So, tell me," she requested, "what the rest of the world is doing."

"Well, Hachi just pulled in a huge contract for his company!" Mari gave her fiancé's arm a squeeze. "I'm so proud of him."

Hachi insisted it wasn't that big a deal, but Yuriko could see that it was. She congratulated him enthusiastically.

"And," Mari continued, "we have a new production assistant on the show."

"You're working on the new quiz show now, right?" Yuriko asked.

"Yes, the one with the stupid costumes...you remember? Well, this one's a Type 1 and I bet it won't be long before she snaps. We actually have a betting pool. I bet that she'd go before the end of her second week."

"Mine's Type 2, but this week was so tough, I bet I get a new one for next week." Yuriko grinned.

Hachi looked back and forth between the two women. "What do you mean by 'Type 1' and 'Type 2'?" he inquired.

Mari laughed into her glass. "It's an idea Yuriko had a while back. You know how...disposable...PAs are, right?" Hachi nodded and Mari continued. "Well, Yuriko says that they seem to break down into three types."

"Type 1," Yuriko took over, "begin as perky and move into hysterical then then finish up homicidal. In their late phases, they chain smoke, drink constantly and talk to themselves alot. Type 2 begin as laconic, or melancholic, and end up suicidal. They simply disappear one day and never return. Type 3s begin and end burnt out. They go from job to job like automatons, with no free will."

"But what about the ones who don't snap or burn out?" Hachi asked. Both women looked at him with complete seriousness and shook their heads.

"No such animal," Yuriko commented. "If it doesn't destroy them, they aren't PAs."

Mari added, "The ones with any real talent leave almost immediately for a better job, a few sleep their way out of the position, but a real PA is one of the above."

"Oh," Hachi said, enlightened.

"Speaking of sleeping with someone, where's Mira tonight?" Mari turned to Yuriko. "I thought you'd bring her."

"Mira?" Yuriko paused, her glass halfway to her mouth. "Who?"

Mari's brows drew together in confusion. "You know - Mira. That Greek reporter you had a fling with last year? She's in town this weekend. I saw her at the studio and told her to give you a call..." Mari paused, taking in Yuriko's puzzled face. "You haven't checked your phone messages, have you?"

"Uh, no, actually..." Yuriko set her glass down and rubbed the back of her head. "I've been so busy and tired when I do get home that..." Looking down at the table, then back at her friend, the blonde asked, "How long did she say she'd be here?"

"She's flying home tomorrow morning," Mari answered, and watched Yuriko sigh. "Sorry."

"No," Yuriko said placidly, "it's just the perfect end to this week." She picked up her glass and drank it dry.

***

At least dinner had been very good, Yuriko thought, as she returned home. And the waitress *was* cute. She looked down at the card she had slipped Yuriko with the check. Tucking the card in her inside pocket, Yuriko grinned. Maybe she'd give her a call sometime.

At home the answering machine blinked twenty times. Yuriko counted - twice. Without hesitation she reached down and hit "erase," then proceeded directly to bed. Alone.

***

ust Relax

he alarm hadn't rung. Yuriko smiled into the pillow happily, lazing in the omfort of her bed, for a solid second before she shot up in a panic. She vas late! Halfway to the bathroom before she realized this was Sunday, 'uriko paused, not sure whether to go back to bed, or just get up. A glance t the clock convinced her that bed was the appropriate choice. She was sleep before her entire body was prostrate.

he room was dark. The weather outside must have been awful. Yuriko miled. Good. She yawned hugely and indulged in a long and luxurious tretch. Rolling over, she mourned the absence of a gorgeous Greek eporter from her bed, then got over it. Sunday. Never before had that vord meant so much to her. She reviewed her plans for the day.

Let's see," she said out loud for the sake of the plants which lined the vindowsill, "today... first call Kishi-san." Yuriko grinned as she pulled the blinds up and looked out upon a dismal gray day. "She's probably chewing ails...I think she owes me a favor, though. I'll get her to send me some-ne to clean this place." Looking down at one plant, she grinned at it. Maybe someone cute."

urning, she left the bedroom, and wandered into the kitchen area. She put vater on for tea, grabbed a package of English tea biscuits and a hunk of heese, plopped them on the counter and hunted through the drawer for a en. In between cutting slices of cheese and laying them on crackers, she vrote herself a list.

'First," she said, her mouth full of cracker and cheese, "Kishi-san." She ;lanced at the clock. Nine-thirty. She'd call in half an hour. By then

Kishi'd have had her morning coffee and be slightly less prickly.

The water was boiling. With plate of crackers and cheese and cup of tea, Yuriko seated herself at the counter. "Second," she sipped the tea, "bath...long bath." She sighed again at the thought of missed opportunities "Third..." she paused, looking around the apartment. She shrugged. "Homework, I guess." She made a face at the list. "Bleah."

Aya-san had done a number on her yesterday, so in addition to her regular classwork, she had extra Japanese work for her tutor. What joy.

"Anything else?" she asked the room at large. Her eyes fell on the pile of love letters. "Oh." She took a deep breath. What the hell was she going to do with those things? Ah well, she'd leave them for later.

"Fourth," she said decisively, "scripts." There must be a better offer than playing a high-school kid in the pile. She finished her tea and crackers, brought her dishes into the kitchen. Looking at the full sink, she resigned herself to at least a little housekeeping. By the time she had dried and put away the last cup, it was time to call her agent.

"Kishi," the gruff voice said. "Whaddaya want?"

Yuriko laughed; she could just *see* her agent, neck deep in paperwork, sucking on cigarettes and pretending that her clients weren't the reason for her having a job in the first place.

"I'm just checking in!" she said, extra perkily. She could practically hear Kishi's teeth grind across the phone lines.

"It's about time." The sound of Kishi sucking in a lungful of nicotine. "Don't you answer messages anymore?"

"I'm sorry." Yuriko imbued her voice with as much genuine apology as she could. "This assignment has been *really* time consuming..." Kishi's snort didn't faze her at all. "And my answering machine seems to be bro-

ken." She stuck her tongue out at the phone. Take that, you old hag.

"Can I ask a favor?" Yuriko's voice was sugary. "Can you hire someone to drop by my place, say twice a week, and give it a cleaning? School and clubs take up all my time these days."

Kishi grunted, which Yuriko took for an affirmative. Having got what she wanted, Yuriko was all sweetness and light, her voice conciliatory as she acquiesced to her agency's every demand. She set her media schedule for the next week - paying close attention that she not be pulled from math class this time - and was ready to ring off, when an idea struck her.

"Kishi-san, I wonder, I have a small problem - maybe you can give me some advice about it."

She could hear the sound of the older woman choking and waited the sarcasm out politely. At last Kishi asked her what it was.

"Well, not surprisingly, I've been getting a lot of love letters…" she raised her voice over the sound of her agent's laughter, "and I'm not sure what to do with them. Any suggestions?"

"Sure," Kishi gloated, "Pick the cutest one for your prom date."

Yuriko's eyes narrowed. "Very funny."

"Okay, okay, I'll see what I can do about it…I'll talk to the kids who answer your fan mail."

Yuriko let out a grateful sigh. "Thanks Kishi-san. I really appreciate it."

The agent sucked in another lungful of tobacco, exhaled and said, "Don't overwork."

Yuriko smiled at the phone and said, "Thanks. I won't." But Kishi had already hung up.

***

Yuriko was a bath enthusiast. When she had first moved out of her family's home, she had lived in a flophouse with three other kids, all with no job, no means of support, and no running water. That relationship hadn't lasted long. Her next residence had been an apartment shared with a drag queen bar hostess, who had hogged their small shower. When she hit it big, the one thing she swore she'd have was a big old bathtub in her bathroom. And so she had. The apartment she now rented had rooms that were of average size, but at some point the owner had pulled down the wall to one of the two bedrooms and made the bathroom insanely luxurious; tiled walls with a mosaic patterned trim…huge frosted glass windows let in a lot of light…and the enormous, plenty big enough for two, furo. Yuriko had fallen in love with the bath at first sight. She sighed happily and leaned back, letting the water rise to her chin.

She loved the way her pale skin turned red after a soak in the tub - she lifted an arm to gaze at the vaguely lobster-like coloring she had taken on. She knew she should get on with her homework, but it all seemed so distant.

"I mean really," she said out loud. *It's utterly ludicrous that I'm worried about my grades*, she continued the thought, sighing now in irritation.

Rising from the tub, she wrapped herself in a towel, slipped her feet into fluffy pink slippers and scuffed her way into the bedroom.

A few minutes later, she reentered the dining room, dressed in jeans, oversized t-shirt and slippers. Seating herself at the table, she frowned down at her book bag. She pulled out her notebook and opened it at random.

"Translate the following passages into English. Please pay particular attention to the use of prepositions..." Gritting her teeth, she began to work.

***

Three down. Yuriko picked up the phone and made a quick call. Five minutes later, she was out the door. The rain had stopped, but the air was heavy with moisture. *That's all right,* she thought. Rainy

Name: Uto Kazuhiko

Birthday: November 13

Zodiac Sign: Scorpio

Blood Type: B

Occupation: Punk

Favorite Color: Silver

Favorite Food: Pancakes

Favorite Music: Rap

Least Favorite Thing: Police, School

day and Sunday it might be, be she would not be gotten down today.

***

Yuriko kicked the door open, holding her takeout bag in her teeth. Keeping her hands away from the doorknob, she elbowed the door shut and bent to drop the bag on the table.

Some takeout, a pile of scripts to read, and newly polished nails. "Life is very good," she announced to the whole world, smiling at her own contentment. "I'm simply gross today." she laughed at her mood.

She seated herself on the sofa, opened one of the scripts and began to shove sushi into her face. It may be ultimately meaningless, she thought, but life really *was* pretty good.

***

The Mysterious Bentou

The day was simply beautiful, Yuriko thought with some irritation. The air was clear, the breeze warm, with an underlying hint of colder weather to come, and the leaves were brilliant shades of gold and red. So nice was it, that she asked the driver to leave her off several blocks away from the school. A walk would clear her head.

She checked her watch, noting that she'd be on time for cleaning duty. One less thing to worry about, at least. She took a deep breath, trying to settle her stomach and calm her nerves. It wasn't like her to feel this way, at all. Maybe Sawako-sensei and his reign of terror was getting to her, after all.

The path to the school was free of distraction. Uto and his gang didn't get here this early, apparently. Pity, some badinage might have taken her mind off her fidgetiness. She spotted the cameraman, Namba, leaning against the school wall, smoking. When he caught sight of her, he lifted the camera. Giving him a second or two to start filming, Yuriko pasted a smile on her face and waved at him. He didn't wave back.

She came closer, looked around for a moment and asked, "Where's, um..." For the life of her, she couldn't recall the PA's name. Namba leaned away from the camera and gave her a crooked smile.

"Gone. New one should be here any minute."

"I called that one right," Yuriko laughed.

Namba nodded. "We all called that one." He paused the film, and lowered the camera. Leaning forward, he spoke sotto voce. "That math teacher of yours caught her later in the hall, too. Said some really harsh stuff. Watch out for him - he's a bastard, he'll look to hurt you if he can."

Yuriko made a face. "Yeah, I know it. Thanks for the warning, though." She caught sight of a figure conspicuously not in uniform making her way towards them. She was a late-stage Type 3 this time. Her hair looked as if it barely saw a comb, her eyes were already glazed and defeated first thing in the morning. Yuriko forgot her name instantly. Two weeks, tops. Namba pulled the cigarette from his mouth, dropped it on the ground and crushed it out. A passing teacher shot him a scathing look. Flushing slightly, he bent down, picked up the offending item and tossed it into a trashcan. Turning, he followed Yuriko and the PA into the school.

Opening her shoe locker, Yuriko found herself confronted with a bizarre sight. She cocked her head at a *bentou* box, neatly tied in a lily-themed paper, that sat in front of her school shoes. How very odd. She pulled the box out, turned it around, then over, but there was no message to be seen, no note, cryptic or otherwise. Love letters were one thing, but love lunches? Yuriko shrugged, and slipped the box into her bag. Probably one of the kids in class trying to be nice.

She pondered the mysterious bentou box as she headed to her classroom. Lilies. Whoever made it was clever, anyway. She slid the door to her classroom open.

***

Cleaning didn't take as long as she thought, but then, Yuriko was pretty sure the other kids were working doubly hard so she didn't have to. Perversely, it made her want to hold up her end of the task. She attacked the floor with unusual vigor. With a laugh at her own contrariness, she thought that if she were half this motivated at home, she wouldn't need someone to clean the place for her.

She did manage to learn the name of the boy who had avoided Aya that day at lunch. Jun was his name, Yamazaki Jun. He seemed unremarkable, but Yuriko watched him surreptitiously while she cleaned, wondering what lay between him and Aya. When cleaning was finished and the other students began to arrive, Yuriko saw Aya flush as she passed him, but neither of them made a gesture or spoke a word to each other. Yuriko found her curiosity piqued.

Sayaka and Aya entered together, and Yuriko greeted them. Noting that her "sempai" was yawning and looked a little tired, Yuriko teased her about her weekend on the town, but Sayaka bore it with good grace. Abe-sensei arrived, looking rattier than ever. Yuriko noticed deep bruise-like spots under his eyes, and a general pallor in his complexion. She turned to Sayaka to whisper, "Doesn't Abe-sensei look terrible? I wonder what *his* weekend was like." Sayaka giggled, but Yuriko noticed his eyes on her, and she pretended not to have been the cause of the girl's outburst.

***

Yuriko found herself staring down at the bentou box she'd found in her locker. She looked up as Sayaka, Aya and a new girl, introduced to her as Mie, joined her at the table.

"Mie is in the writing club," Sayaka explained, "but she was out sick when you met us last week."

Yuriko introduced herself to the young girl, trying not to laugh at the stars in her eyes.

"I was so sad to have been out last week," Mie said, practically inaudibly. "When I heard you were coming to our school I couldn't believe it!"

Yuriko smiled pleasantly, ignoring the clenching of her stomach. Fangirls always gave her a weird feeling. It was nice to be popular, but there was something about the way they looked at you...like they possessed you. It was always kind of creepy.

Mie glanced down at the bentou box in front of Yuriko and practically squealed with delight. "It's so cu-u-ute!"

Yuriko looked at Sayaka, who grinned a little nastily at her. "It is cute, Yuriko-kun...did you make it?"

Yuriko shook her head. "No. Actually...I was going to ask you if you did."

Sayaka shook her head, so Yuriko glanced at Aya, who looked puzzled.

"Where did you get it, then?" Aya asked.

"I don't know," Yuriko said honestly. "It was in my locker this morning when I arrived."

"Oooohhh, a mystery!" Sayaka said and clasped her hands together. "Who do you think it is?"

Mie pouted. "I wish I had thought of it. Oh, Yuriko-san, can I make you lunch tomorrow?" Her eyes fairly pulsed with hearts.

A little nonplussed, Yuriko begged off. "Um, I think I can handle it myself, hanks. But I appreciate the offer."

"Maybe," Aya said in a hissed stage whisper, "Sawako-sensei left it and it's actually poisoned!" She laughed happily at her own joke. Yuriko lifted an eyebrow at her.

"The thought had crossed my mind," she said dryly.

"Open it," Mie squeaked, "open it! Let's see if it's as cute inside too!"

Yuriko shrugged, and opened the wrapping to find an average, plastic bentou box inside. She opened it and the girls crowded around, cooing at the nicely arranged rice balls, Vienna sausages and other delicious-looking tidbits.

"It has a nicely homemade look, but there is a sense of composition, too," Yuriko declared, "an almost expressionistic quality." The other girls laughed.

"Do you always critique your lunches?" Sayaka asked.

"My friend Mari and I do, yes. We got into the habit at the studio canteen. The food there is so...inedible, that it begs to be treated as a kind of postmodern nihilistic art form." Sayaka and Aya thought this hysterical, but Mie simply gave Yuriko a puzzled, albeit besotted, smile. Yuriko sighed internally. "Let's eat, shall we?" she suggested.

***

It was a good lunch; Yuriko was impressed. Better than her own feeble attempts at cooking, by far. When mealtime was over, she carefully washed the box, dried it and tucked the cloth inside. Placing them in her locker, she turned away, then had a second thought. Pulling out pen and paper, she jotted a note and stuck it in the box with the wrapper. "Thanks. It was extremely tasty and very considerate. Love, Yuriko." Whistling happily, she went back to class.

Volume 1, Issue 12

Brewing up a Storm

Yuriko stopped outside Matsumori-sensei's office, her hand lifted to knock at the doorframe. She could see two figures in the small room. One was Matsumori-sensei herself, sitting at her desk. It took Yuriko a moment longer to recognize the other woman. Having never seen Kaori smiling, it was a few seconds before Yuriko could associate the laughing girl she now saw with the dour and intense figure she was familiar with. Yuriko let her hand fall as she observed the two.

Kaori was sitting on the edge of the desk, her head thrown back in laughter. Color gave her face a lively look, and her eyes sparkled as she spoke to the coach. Her hair was unbound, and fell thickly along her back - she was a very pretty girl already, but in five years, she'd be a knockout. Her body was athletic and her natural grace already apparent. Someone's heart would be turned to dust by Kaori pretty soon if she wasn't careful.

Smiling at the thought, Yuriko knocked lightly on the door. Kaori's reaction was instant. She leapt from the desk edge and stood uncomfortably. Upon identifying the intruder, her face underwent a remarkable change. The color in her cheeks faded and her eyes, which had been alight with pleasure, grew cold and hard. Bowing towards Matsumori-sensei, she excused herself. As they passed, Yuriko greeted Kaori warmly, but received no more than a grunt and the barest nod in return. Both of the older women watched as the girl left the office, every muscle in her body held rigidly.

"Whew..." Yuriko said, "is that an icy wind I feel? Did I ever do something to her that I don't remember?"

Matsumori-sensei's face was sad and a little serious as she answered. "I

don't think so, but I think you'd better look elsewhere to make friends.
Kaori-kun is a lovely girl - dedicated, focused and very, very talented. Her
blood type is A, you know."

Yuriko nodded. "I would have guessed that. I'm an 'O,' myself."

The coach laughed. "I would have guessed that."

"So, Matsumori-sensei..." Yuriko began.

"Ruriko, please." The woman smiled. "I feel strange having you be so for-
mal with me. I feel like we've known each other a long time."

"So, you're a type AB, then," Yuriko laughed.

"Got it in one!" The coach confirmed. "Well, there's two things, actually. I
spoke to the principal and the school basketball league board... and

you're right. They won't allow you to play in games."

Yuriko shrugged. "I'm not surprised." She forbore mentioning how relieved she was. School was exhausting enough without having to be on a competition training schedule.

"So, I've decided to let you only come to practice twice a week," Ruriko-sensei continued.

Yuriko found herself sighing with relief. "I can't thank you enough for that! My agent is beginning to think that I'm ignoring her out of spite. Now I'll have an extra evening to schedule interviews and auditions." She ran her hand through her hair. "That's a huge favor, thank you."

Ruriko-sensei gave her a nasty grin. "I wasn't finished. In return I need a favor from you." The coach leaned forward with that conspiratorial air Yuriko liked so much.

Behind the camera, Namba knew enough to pan away, pulling himself out of the office...he might miss the dialogue, but the mystery would make a great ending to an episode. Cliffhangers sold. He filmed from outside the office, through the window. Yuriko listened to the teacher with a look of extreme surprise, then began to laugh. *Perfect,* Namba thought. *Just perfect.*

***

"So, we hear you have a new project in the works." The deejay sounded like he had a head cold.

Yuriko adjusted the awkward earphones and imbued her voice with a warm smile. "Yes, and it's very exciting."

"Can you tell us about it?" The deejay looked as bored as Yuriko felt.

"Only a little. It's a new "reality" TV show...I'm going back to high

chool to relive the 'springtime of
youth.'"

"Oh," the deejay said unconvincingly,
"that sounds like fun."

"It is!" Yuriko hoped she sounded more
enthusiastic than she felt. "After all, who
wouldn't want to relive the best years of
their lives?"

Mari was waiting for her with a can of
tea. Yuriko juggled the can as Mari
tossed it, trying to keep it off the floor.

"'The best years of their lives'?" Mari
asked, incredulously.

Yuriko grimaced. "Kishi-san told me to
say that. I think it's one of the possible
titles for the show. 'The Best Years of
Our Lives' or something like that."

Mari nodded, sipping from her own can.
"How horrible."

Yuriko nodded, distractedly.

"Hey," Mari asked, "are you okay, Yuri?
You seem kind of out of it."

Yuriko blinked a few times. "I don't
know. I've been feeling edgy all day. I'm
not sure why."

Mari grinned. "Big test coming up that

Name: Izumi Aya

Birthday: December 17

Zodiac Sign: Capricorn

Blood Type: A

Occupation: Honor Student,
Tutor

Favorite Color: Purple

Favorite Food: Takoyaki

Favorite Music: Show Tunes

Least Favorite Thing:
Milk, People Who Are
Always Late

you haven't studied for?"

Yuriko stuck her tongue out at her friend. "Funny."

Mari threaded her arm through Yuriko's. "Come on, I'll treat for dinner. The canteen has an exciting new Dadaist dish you'll like."

Yuriko laughed. "It sounds appetizing."

"Probably not." Mari smiled and dragged her friend off towards the canteen.

***

Yuriko pushed some of the unidentifiable food around on her plate. "I like the lack of color - very washed out."

"Yes," Mari agreed. "A distinct muted feel. It cries out in pain."

"So will we, if we eat it," Yuriko pronounced, shoving the plate away. She gazed around the crowded room. People in fruit costumes sat at one table, a samurai walked by with a tray of food. A new idol group were whispering in one corner - they looked twelve; okay, maybe fourteen. She sighed.

"I feel like...like I don't belong here anymore." Yuriko said suddenly.

Mari stared at her friend in surprise. "You don't mean that, do you?"

"Yes, actually, I do. It's only been a week, but..."

Mari gave Yuriko a hard look. "Yuri..."

Yuriko looked abashed. "I'm sorry. I guess I'm just tired."

Mari smiled at her friend. "Keep the faith, Yuriko. Even bad jobs come to an end." When Yuriko gave her a small smile, Mari continued, "Now...

ell me more about the girls you sit with. I'm jealous of your new friends."

Yuriko grinned. "Well...one unrequited love and one mysterious relation-ship - oh, and don't let me forget to tell you about the magical, mysterious lunch!"

The two friends chatted away, while around them the crowd ebbed and flowed.

***

Volume 1, Issue 13

The Center Cannot Hold

Yuriko hesitated before lifting the door to her shoe locker. Love letters, mysterious lunches - what will today's toy surprise be? she wondered. But nothing fell out, so she looked under the flap. Today's bentou box was wrapped with a little flourish at the top, in a cherry blossom-patterned *furoshiki*.

"Okay," she said, "I sense a trend." Sticking the box in her bag, she proceeded to homeroom for cleaning duty. Today she made an effort to chat up Jun, hoping to learn a little bit about him - and by extension, Aya - but she found the boy taciturn and unresponsive. One of the other boys whispered to her later that Jun had not too long ago lost an older brother and that he hadn't been the same since. Yuriko pondered this tidbit as she cleaned.

Sayaka found Yuriko sitting at her desk chewing on a pencil, lost in thought. The girl stood for a moment looking down at the blonde, then began to chuckle. Yuriko stared at her for a moment in confusion, smiling unsurely.

"What's so amusing?" she asked.

Sayaka gestured at Yuriko's hands. "It's not often one sees polished nails and the boy's uniform together on the same person."

"Oh, that," Yuriko said blandly.

Sayaka looked concerned. "Are you alright?"

Yuriko spoke as if she hadn't heard the other girl. "Do you know anything about Aya-san? I mean, about her family or anything?"

Sayaka looked around to see who might hear. "Not much, but," she looked around again and lowered her voice, leaning towards Yuriko, "I heard that her sister died some time ago. She was pregnant and the baby died too. Her family is very overprotective of her now."

"Oh." Was there some connection there? Maybe they died in the same accident? Or maybe… Yuriko's train of thought was interrupted by the girl's appearance. She greeted Aya, but watched her closely for anything unusual.

"Did you get another lunch box today?" Aya asked brightly.

Yuriko nodded. "It seems to be my lucky week."

They rose for the teacher. Abe-sensei looked as if he'd slept in his clothes…or, more likely, not slept at all. Yuriko was beginning to feel concerned for the man. Ratty and bewildered was one thing, but this…. To add to her feeling of discomfort, every time she looked at the front of the class, his eyes were there, boring into her own. Yuriko spent most of homeroom studying the surface of her desk.

***

Sayaka glanced at Yuriko again. The blonde seemed a little distracted today. She nudged Yuriko with her foot and watched with surprise as the older woman's head snapped up.

"She's called you twice," Sayaka hissed under her breath. Yuriko apologized to the English teacher, stood and read the passage. Sitting down once again, she mouthed "Thank you" to Sayaka, who just nodded.

"What is *with* you today?" the girl asked after the teacher left.

Yuriko shook her head. "I'm not sure, I feel funny. Like I don't fit my skin."

"Oh well, welcome to high school." Sayaka said lightly.

Yuriko smiled. "No. I mean, I know what you mean and maybe you're right. Maybe it's just because I'm back in school, but...."

"Could it be that all the old insecurities are popping up?" Sayaka asked.

Yuriko thought about that, then shook her head. "No - it's not that." She paused. "But I don't know what it is," she finished lamely.

Sayaka decided to change the subject. "I wanted to ask you before. The writing and art clubs are going out today after school to enjoy the changing of the leaves. We'd like it very much if you joined us."

Yuriko rocked her head back and forth as she considered. "I'd like that, but...I'll have to leave a little early. I have a prior appointment."

Sayaka assured her that it would be fine. "Don't forget to bring paper - we're composing *haiku*!"

"Of course we are," Yuriko said acerbically.

***

It was a nice outing. The art students sketched while the writing club traded impromptu haiku. Yuriko laid back on the grass and watched the light overhead flicker through the leaves. She let the cadence of the extemporaneous poetry soothe her frayed nerves.

"What about you, Yuriko-san?" a male voice asked. She cracked an eye open and turned her head. Ogawa, the writing club vice president, was leaning over her with a pleasant grin.

Yuriko yawned slightly and sat up. "What about me?" she inquired.

"Well, we were wondering if you had a haiku to share with us."

Yuriko looked around her, at all the young faces that watched her in antici-pation. Several of the art club members had ceased to sketch and now hung on her every word. Inexpressable sadness welled up in her for a moment.

She put her hands behind her head and forced a grin. "I have two - which one do you want?"

"The dirty one!" one of the boys in the art club shouted. They all laughed.

Yuriko put her hand up to quiet the crowd. "The first one." She cleared her throat. "A breeze on my cheek / the gentle breath of the sky / as you stroke my face." The girls all sighed audibly with longing. Yuriko jumped, remembering where she was and with whom. "Oh, sorry," she said sheep-ishly. "I meant the leaves, of course, when they fall."

"Of course," Ogawa said graciously.

"Second," Yuriko said, pulling her legs under her and taking a deep breath. "The burning ember/ the sun's last moment of life/ ignites the forest."

The general consensus was that Yuriko wasn't bad at impromptu haiku.

Mie closed the distance between them and looked up at Yuriko with a puppy dog-like expression. "That haiku was so-o-o beautiful!" she cooed.

Yuriko gave the girl a cold smile as she stood. "Thank you."

Turning to the rest of the students, Yuriko made her apologies, reminding Sayaka that she had to leave. Picking up her book bag, one hand in her pocket, Yuriko wandered along the paths through the trees towards the street.

Behind her on the grass several pairs of eyes followed her. One pair were concerned, one were filled with fantasies and one, gazing in the direction she went the longest, were filled with too many emotions to express.

Volume 1, Issue 14

Melt Down

"It was the weirdest thing," Yuriko sipped at her coffee and sat back in her chair. Mariko had the world's largest collection of comfortable chairs in her apartment.

"So, what exactly happened?" Mari inquired.

"Well, I told you about Abe-sensei, right? My homeroom and science teacher? He looks kind of rumpled, like a shirt that was left under a pile of other clothes for a long time." Both women grinned at the image. "But this week he hasn't been rumpled - he's been fraying at the edges. He looks as if he hasn't gotten any sleep at all. And I swear, every time I look up he's staring at me with this hungry look. It was really creeping me out."

"But I thought you said you thought he was..." Mari said.

"I did think so, but now I wonder." Yuriko sipped her coffee again. "Mmm, this is really good. Just what I needed, thanks."

Mari preened. "Always glad to provide what's needed."

Yuriko raised an eyebrow, but said nothing. Mari poked her in the arm to get her talking again.

"So, this morning, when he comes in, he looks like hell. I thought he might keel over in homeroom, he looked so bad." Yuriko paused. "I really felt bad for him, but the weird thing was..." she tapered off.

"That's twice now you've said that and stopped," Mari insisted. "*What* was the weird thing?"

"Well...I seem to be the only one who noticed," Yuriko said. "None of the kids even looked at him strangely. And Sayaka, who seems to have a good head on her shoulders, when I asked her if he'd been acting funny, she just shrugged."

"Maybe he's a drinker and this is just another binge." Mariko suggested, as she stood to pour more coffee. Yuri handed her cup over eagerly.

"Maybe," Yuriko admitted. "So, anyway, come science class, Abe-sensei is late, then very late and, at last, almost thirty minutes into the class, the principal walks in and says that Abe-sensei has had an emergency at home and had to leave early."

"Maybe his...whatever…was sick."

"Maybe," Yuriko repeated. "I don't know, though...."

The two women sat in silence for a while. Mari watched her friend with some concern. Usually a natty dresser, she had come over in a worn sweatshirt, and her face looked a little drawn. Mariko put her cup down.

"Yuri - you're not looking so well yourself. It's nice that you are working hard at this assignment, but..." Mariko wasn't sure exactly what it was that she was worried about.

Yuriko grinned. "I'm fine, really. I came straight here from basketball practice. I'm just tired."

"Oh, how is basketball practice?" Mariko asked, her eyebrow lifted suggestively.

Yuriko waved away the implication. "If they were five years older, it'd be a whole different story. I feel like I'm working out with younger cousins." She laughed. "Only they treat me like I'm their junior, which in a sense I am - it makes for a strange dynamic."

"Any warming on the cold front?"

"You mean Yamamoto Kaori-buchou?" Yuriko asked. "No. Icy as ever. Luckily for me one Noda Mikan is the vice-captain, and she's in charge of my training. Nice kid, bluff, strong, treats me like an equal. She's probably going to figure out she's gay in three years, spend ten in bad relationships, and resign herself to a life of coaching sports and living with her cats."

Mariko choked on her coffee. "Yuri!" she laughed, scandalized.

"Well, it's the truth," the blonde said unrepentantly. She set her empty coffee cup down. "So tell me, how's Hachi?"

Something odd passed through Mari's eyes for a second, but she smiled brightly. "Oh, he's just fine. Busy." She waved her hand vaguely.

Yuriko looked at her stonily. "Hayashi Mariko, don't try to pull one over on me. What's up?"

Mari waved her concern away flightily. "It's really nothing - he's just been busy this week, with that new account. We haven't had much of a chance to talk, that's all."

Yuriko sat back again, nodding. "Feeling lonely?" She stretched out in the chair, extending her long legs in front of her. "I can understand that. So does Hachi. Just make sure he makes up for it, with interest," she grinned.

Mari returned the smile easily. "Oh! I forgot to tell you. I was in the ice cream parlor - you know, the one around the corner from the studio - and I saw a few girls from your school. They were talking about you."

Yuriko groaned. "What now?"

"No, no, nothing like that. One girl was praising you to the heavens. How gorgeous you are, how polite and funny - and that you write exceptional haiku."

Yuriko rolled her eyes. "About this tall?" She held her hand at mid-chest level. "Short, dark hair in a bob? Big eyes with stars in them?"

Mari nodded. "You know her?"

Yuriko rolled her eyes again. "Ohhhh, yes. Her name is Mie, she's in the writing club… and she has an enormous fangirl crush." Yuriko rubbed her face in frustration. "I just hope she doesn't make any trouble."

"She didn't look like much. Is she that bad?"

"Probably not," Yuriko admitted. "But there's something about her - some special quality of insipidity that really worries me."

Mariko smirked. "Start working on your polite rejection speech now…"

Yuriko nodded. "Exactly."

Mariko checked her watch, then stood. "And now I'm kicking you out. You have school tomorrow." She gave Yuriko a goofy grin. "And I'm sure you have homework to do."

Yuriko rose a little stiffly. "Ohhhh! All this sports activity is killing me." Mari laughed at her moans and unsympathetically hustled her to the door.

"Be careful, Yuri," Mariko said as her friend opened the door. "These kids have real feelings, you know."

"I do know," Yuriko insisted. "I wonder if they realize that about me."

Mari closed the door behind the blonde, and thought about that last comment for a long time.

***

Name: Yamamoto Kaori

Birthday: January 18

Zodiac Sign: Capricorn

Blood Type: A

Occupation: Captain of the Basketball Team, Honor Student

Favorite Color: Violet

Favorite Food: Oden

Favorite Music: J-Rock

Least Favorite Thing: Art Class

Return to Zero

Yuriko finished putting away the cleaning equipment and headed for her seat. She could hear some of the early arrivers chatting amongst themselves. They appeared to be discussing some new pop group. Pop music wasn't her gig; she sang it, but didn't like it much.

As she passed, one of the girls called out to her, followed quickly by the others. She stopped and smiled down at them.

"Yuriko-san," a slightly heavy girl asked her, "you like music, right?"

Yuriko nodded pleasantly.

"What's your favorite song?" a girl with very long hair asked.

"Elgar's *Cello Concerto in E Minor.*"

The girls found this hysterical. When they stopped giggling, the heavy one said, "No, really, Yuriko-san. What's your favorite?"

Yuriko looked at her, puzzled. "That *is* my favorite."

For a solid second, there was dead silence, then the long-haired girl broke in. "But you know that new band, right? The Threetones?"

Yuriko shook her head slowly. "I don't...oh, wait! Are they three girls, they look twelve, all have nose pierces?"

The girls all nodded enthusiastically.

"Well," Yuriko admitted, "I've never actually heard them. I just saw them at the studio last week."

The girls boggled at her. "At the studio…?" the heavy girl asked.

"Well, sure. I had to check in, see my agent, do an interview…" Yuriko stopped as she realized what she was saying. The girls stared at her wide-eyed and starstruck all over again. She sighed internally.

Then, smiling brightly, she came up with a brilliant suggestion. "Hey, I have to stop by again in a week or so - would you like to see the studio? I can probably arrange for a tour…" the cries of delight drowned out her last words. In mere seconds every new person entering the class was informed of the tour…and Yuriko was beating herself up for opening her big mouth. She slunk over to her desk, nodding politely to anyone who asked a question.

Aya entered and came directly over. "Is it true?"

Yuriko looked up wildly. "What? That I'm losing my mind? Definitely."

Aya giggled. "No, that you've offered to take us on a tour of your studio."

"Oh, that." Yuriko waved nonchalantly. "I actually offered to set up a tour, but the way my luck is running, I'll be leading it myself." Looking at the cameraman who stood immediately on her left, filming a close-up, she had a thought and buried her face in her arms. "And they'll film it, won't they?"

Aya patted her shoulder shyly. "It won't be that bad, I'm sure."

Yuriko thanked her and waved as Sayaka entered.

The girl waved back as she came over. "I've already heard." She smiled. "You're very impulsive, you know?"

Yuriko looked at her seriously. "You sound just like my friend Mariko."

"You talk about her quite a bit - how long have you been friends?" Sayaka looked thoughtful.

"Since we were kids," Yuriko said. "We were neighbors when we were very little." She smiled gently. "We've been close from way back. Someday I'll introduce you. I think you'd like her, and vice versa."

When Abe-sensei entered, Yuriko took a long, relieved breath. He didn't look any worse - and maybe even a very little better. At least he didn't look as if he'd slept in his clothes, and his face wasn't gray anymore. She sent up a general sort of prayer for him, just glad that he hadn't gone and done anything rash. In the end,Mariko was probably right , he must have just had an illness in the family.

When he called her name, Yuriko smiled at Abe-sensei and was rewarded with the tiniest of smiles in return. No, Mari was most likely right after all

**

It's been a long week, Yuriko thought, *but at least Sawako-sensei hasn't been overtly hostile.* After last Saturday's blow-up, he seemed to have calmed down to a low simmer. Class wasn't any easier, but he seemed to have tired of abusing her specifically.

Until today. By the time math class was over, Yuriko had a pounding headache in the middle of her forehead. He had called her to the board eight times. She had gotten six of the problems right, but he still didn't seem satisfied. She blew out a frustrated breath and rubbed her temples as she sat for the last time. She wondered if she had any aspirin on her and decided that she probably didn't.

When class ended, Sawako-sensei called Yuriko up to the front of the room. Bristling at her from under heavy brows, he spoke to her in a low,

reatening tone. "If you think you can get through my class without
vorking, you're wrong."

he bit back the reply that sprang to her lips. Clearing her throat she said,
I'll do my best," and gave him a thin smile.

Iis face grew tight, his lips pursed and he stared hard at her. "That won't
e good enough," he said, and dismissed her.

he sank back down in her seat, defeated.

***

So, what's for lunch today?" Aya asked brightly.

uriko held up today's mystery lunch. "Feels like a sandwich."

She hefted the box a bit.

"And you still don't know who's leaving them?" Aya was amazed. "You'll have to come to school at the crack of dawn to find out."

"I am asleep at the crack of dawn," Yuriko said. "And I don't plan on changing that." She unwrapped the bentou, and noted that she had been correct. A very nicely made sandwich greeted her. She picked it up with some relish. "Man, I am so hungry."

"After your workout with Sawako-sensei, I'm not surprised." Sayaka joined them with a tray of food. She placed a can of tea in front of Yuriko and one in front of Aya, then took the last for herself.

"Thanks!" Yuriko said, and took a gulp of the tea. "Whoever it is who's leaving these," she said with a grin, "makes lunch much better than I ever would. I'm grateful to whomever it is."

Three girls walked past Yuriko and she glanced up to smile at them. Two waved slightly, but from the third all she received was a frigid stare.

"Whoa," Aya whispered, "what did you do to Yamamoto-san?"

Yuriko waited until the three girls passed out of hearing. "I honestly don't know!" Her nerves were more frayed than she realized and her voice cracked a little. She sighed. "You'd think I'd seduced her older sister or something."

Without noticing the looks on the two girls' faces, she continued. "Maybe that's it! I hadn't even considered that...does Yamamoto-san have a sister?" She looked from one gaping girl to another, then again, and finally ended with a lame, "What?"

Aya was the first to break. Her eyes were huge and more than a little offended as she stared at Yuriko. "How could you say such a thing?"

"What?" Yuriko asked, a little confused.

Sayaka's reaction was completely different. Her face was red with embarassment as a wave of nervous laughter took over.

Yuriko backtracked in the conversation, then flushed. "Oh, sorry...I wasn't thinking."

Aya stood suddenly. "That was really thoughtless," she said coldly, and left the table.

Yuriko stared after her for a moment, then turned to Sayaka, who was gazing after her as well. "I am sorry," she began, "but what was that all about?"

Sayaka shook her head. "I don't know." Turning to Yuriko, she asked, all gossipy. "Have you really had so many lovers that you can't remember them all?"

Yuriko gazed at the girl. "I'm sorry. I shouldn't have said anything," she apologized.

"But..." Sayaka began.

Yuriko held up a hand to stall her. "No. I'm sorry. We really can't have that conversation. Excuse me." And she stood, bowed, then left, following in Aya's footsteps.

***

Love and Death

Yuriko found Aya sitting alone on the hill that overlooked the school's playing fields. The girl was hugging her knees and staring off into the distance. Yuriko cleared her throat as she approached. Aya looked up, but when she saw who it was she turned her head away.

Bowing deeply, Yuriko offered a sincere apology. "I am very sorry for offending you by my irresponsible remark." She kept her head down until Aya impatiently accepted her apology.

"Do you want to talk about it?" Yuriko asked, approaching the girl slowly.

Aya shrugged. "Not really." She leaned her forehead against her knees. "I'm sorry," she said, her voice muffled against her legs. "I didn't mean to react so strongly."

Yuriko sat herself on the grass, keeping her distance. Pulling her own knees up, she leaned on them, staring out at the fields.

"Where's your tail?" Aya asked, a bit sharply.

"I asked him to go take a cigarette break." Yuriko knew exactly whom Aya meant. "The show is supposed to be about me and my coping skills, not about my friends and their private woes."

Aya sighed. "It's really nothing."

Yuriko turned towards her slightly. "I'm willing to listen anyway."

Aya looked up, her eyes red-rimmed, but dry. "I had an older sister," she said with the slightest stress on the word "had."

"Oh." Yuriko said quietly.

"She died a little less than a year ago." The girl looked away again. "She was pregnant with her lover's child - it died too."

"Oh," Yuriko said again, feeling very stupid and inconsiderate. She remembered Sayaka saying something about this. "I'm sorry."

"When you said...what you said, it made me think of some of the things my parents used to say about her. It's not your fault - you couldn't have known."

"Your parents?" Yuriko asked.

Aya sighed. "We're an old, prestigious family - or so my parents keep insisting. She fell in love below her station. They blamed her lover for seducing her, deceiving her.

"When she returned home pregnant, they nearly imprisoned her in the house. They wouldn't let him see her or talk to her...even though she said she wanted to marry him." The girl fell silent.

"Aya-san - I'm so sorry."

"No, let me finish, because I owe you an apology, as well. When Aika - my sister - died, my parents sent her lover no notice. He was never told. When he found out, he tried to visit her grave, but my parents had him kept out of the cemetery. He went mad with grief and ran away. No one's seen him since. My family blames him - his family blames mine."

Aya stood quickly and bowed. "I apologize for my rude behavior. You didn' know - couldn't have known."

Yuriko accepted the apology and waved the girl back to her seat on the ground. "I offended you unintentionally, and you overreacted - I think we're even."

They sat without speaking for a long time, until the bell for class rang. They stood and walked together back towards the school. Yuriko paused, her hands in her pockets.

"Yamazaki-kun's brother...he was Aika's lover, wasn't he?" she said, at last.

Aya paled. "How did you know that?" she hissed. "Did he tell you?"

Yuriko shook her head. "It was a guess. I'm sorry - I'm being nosey, but I saw the way you two freeze each other out and I just put it together."

Aya began to shake a little, and hugged herself as she walked. "I don't know whether to be relieved or upset, now that someone else knows about that."

Yuriko stopped her and looked down into Aya's face. "A burden shared is a burden halved. It's a platitude, but I believe in it. I won't tell anyone, but if you ever need to talk..."

The girl nodded, and shivered again. Yuriko smiled. "C'mon, let's get back to class." She unbuttoned her jacket and took it off, draping it over the girl's shoulders. "Wear this until we get back inside," she said nonchalantly and began walking again.

Aya watched her walk away. Her cheeks pinked as she jogged to catch up to the long-legged blonde.

***

The bell rang, and Yuriko closed her science book with a sigh. She glanced at the teacher, who nodded and she rose. As she headed for the door, Abe-sensei intercepted her. She stopped to face him.

"I know you have an interview right now, but..." he murmured, "if you have a moment, before you leave today, I'd like a word with you."

Surprised, Yuriko nodded. Abe-sensei gestured for her to precede him through the door.

Name: Matsumori Ruriko

Birthday: February 22

Zodiac Sign: Aquarius

Blood Type: AB

Occupation: High School Gym Teacher

Favorite Color: Green

Favorite Food: Yakitori

Favorite Music: Jazz

Least Favorite Things: Eggs, Television Commericals

She stepped through and almost ran into the principal. He beamed at her and steadied her as she pulled back.

"Good, good. I was just coming to get you!" He looked past her shoulder at Abe-sensei, "And you as well, Abe-sensei. I was hoping that you could come to my office for a moment."

Yuriko could see the teacher's haggard face blanch. "Of course, of course," he stuttered.

Yuriko and the PA followed the two men down the hall. She nodded as the PA rattled on about the next interview, but kept her eye on her homeroom teacher.

***

Yuriko gave her tie a last tug, checked herself in the mirror and opened the front door.

"Am I late?"

"Not at all," Yuriko said. "Let me just grab my coat and we can go."

"I really appreciate this. I've looked around for a while, but I had no idea where to go."

"Oh, no," Yuriko smiled. "It's my great pleasure to assist such a beautiful lady."

"Oh! Aren't you the charmer!"

"Not at all. Just being honest. Well, shall we go," she held the door open. "Ruriko-sensei?"

***

Volume 1, Issue 17

Perseverance

Yuriko awoke smiling. She was feeling happier than she'd been in a while, although she couldn't say why. Perhaps Ruriko-sensei's company had been the cause. She really was a lovely woman - and she danced very well indeed.

Moving briskly through her morning ablutions, Yuriko dressed, gathered her things together for school and was out the door faster than she had been all week.

She walked the last few blocks to school wondering about the sense of general unease that had filled her recently. She couldn't put her finger on it, but she made a resolution to find the answer before the weekend.

***

Abe-sensei was absent. Yuriko had tried to find him yesterday before she left school for the day, but he hadn't been seen since science class. When homeroom was about to begin, the principal entered.

"Abe-sensei has had to take a short leave of absence due to personal concerns. He'll return as soon as possible," the principal's deep voice rumbled. "Until a substitute can be found, science class will be self-study. Thank you for your cooperation." After the principal left, Sato stood and took attendance.

Yuriko turned to Sayaka. "I told you something funny was up with him. Does he drink or anything like that?"

The girl shrugged indifferently. "No - well, not that I know of." She looked at the blonde curiously. "Why do you want to know, anyway?"

"I don't know - there's something about him...."

"Oh," Sayaka said blankly.

Yuriko gave her a hard look. "I'm sorry about running out on you yesterday."

Sayaka kept her eyes on her notebook. "It wasn't that. I could see Aya-san was upset - and I think it was nice of you to go after her. It's just that..." her voice faded out.

"Just what?" asked Yuriko.

Sayaka's face scrunched up a little as she tried to frame her words. "Up until yesterday, you've treated me like an equal. But when I asked you about...you know, all of a sudden, I was just a little kid."

Yuriko was speechless. "I...I don't know what to say. I'm sorry."

Sayaka waved her apology away. "No, you see - you were right. I went home last night and thought about it. You're being really nice to me, calling me sempai and all, but," she paused, "really, you've become my sempai." She looked up and smiled at the older woman. "I realized just how much I look up to you - and we've only known each other two weeks. It surprised me."

Yuriko considered that. "Remember that conversation we had when we met, about me never fitting in? All my life people have had very strong reactions to me, one way or another. My friend Mari's fiancé calls it my "magic power.""

Sayaka laughed at that. "Like Sawako-sensei?"

"Or Yamamoto-san. I've come to rely on it, because without the friends I make, I'd have no family at all." She smiled at the girl. "My friends," Yuriko spoke deliberately, "*are* my family."

Sayaka looked up and met Yuriko's eyes. "Thank you," she said after a moment, then smiled.

***

Today's lunch was a cold noodle dish - it even included two homemade cookies. A few of the girls from the basketball team had joined them for lunch, including Noda Mikan, her team sempai. They all watched the "opening of the bentou" ceremony with great interest and many comments of jealousy.

"I wish someone did that for me!" Mikan said, as she looked at her own ungainly bentou in disapproval.

"Become a famous idol and maybe someone will," another girl said. Mikan made a face.

"So," the third girl asked Aya, "there's been a new lunch every day this week?"

Aya nodded vigorously. "It's the biggest mystery in the school," she said.

"No it's not," contradicted the second girl. Yuriko recalled her name as Emi, from her first day in school. "What happened to Abe-sensei has to be first place."

"Thank you!" Yuriko chimed in. "I figured I couldn't be the *only* one that was worried!"

"Worried?" Mikan asked. "Why would you be worried?"

"Aren't you? He's looking terrible, he disappears..." Yuriko looked from one face to another, but no one looked more than slightly intrigued.

"Maybe, " the third girl, Natsuki, said, "he's having trouble with his wife...or a mistress. Or both."

Most of the heads at the table nodded. "It's probably just something sordid like that," Sayaka commented.

Yuriko looked around again. She'd forgotten this about high school...if it didn't affect you personally, it wasn't important. Oh well, she'd figure that out eventually too. Add it to the growing list of mysteries.

***

Today was the day to go over the writing club interview questions. It had been decided that each member would come up with a question to be asked of Yuriko. The actual interview would take place at the next meeting, presided over by Ogawa and filmed in the school studio by the television crew. Each student spent this meeting formulating the question that would best allow their own and Yuriko's individuality to be expressed in the interview.

All in all, it was a challenging assignment. While most of the club members had heard many media interviews - and knew how boring and lackluster they were - few had ever tried to write for one.

Yuriko pitched in, trying to come up with a question of her own that would best convey herself as a writer - and as a performer. When the club's time came to an end, more than a few heads wagged in regret.

Ogawa handed Yuriko the papers, shaking his own head. "That was a lot tougher than I thought!" He laughed. "I'd better practice that more if I want to be in journalism."

"Is that what you want to do?" Yuriko inquired. The boy nodded.

"Definitely!" His eyes lit up with enthusiasm. Yuriko could see Sayaka trying to listen without being obvious, but she could also see something ayaka could not. Behind the club president stood another member, one who watched her with the same expression the girl had when she watched Ogawa. Yuriko grinned internally. There was nothing she loved more than a challenge.

***

Mari leaned forward earnestly. "So, Yuriko, what led you to show business?"

Yuriko's lip curled. "Really? That's so...average."

Mariko looked at the paper in front of her and shrugged. "They're only high school kids, after all."

Yuri looked down at the paper she held in her hand and read, "'What was one of the defining moments of your life?'" She nodded. "That's not half bad."

Mari agreed. "What *was* one of the defining moments of your life?" she asked curiously.

Yuriko considered. "Well, meeting you was one." She smiled at her friend. "Would you mind if I answered with that story? I think it would make a good answer."

"Sure!" Mari said, and laughed. "It was pretty much one of my defining moments too."

"And then there was the day I met Junko..." Yuriko sighed nostalgically. "And, of course, the day I was thrown out."

Mari nodded slowly. "That was a day, all right. I remember it like it happened yesterday."

"Me too," Yuriko said. She gestured to the pile of questions Mari held.

"Next."

Mari flipped through the next few, looking for one that stood out. "Role model, that's alright, favorite color...oh, wait, here's a really odd one." She pulled out a sheet and read, "'If you could be any kind of material, which would you be?'" Mari pointed to the signature. "Look! It's from your little fan, Mie."

Yuriko shuddered, but thought about the question. "Silk," she answered at last.

Mari raised an eyebrow. "Would you care to elaborate on that?"

"No," Yuriko said firmly and shot her a look.

"Aren't we all uptight?" Mariko teased. "When was the last time you went out on a real date, anyway?"

Yuriko stared at her friend in surprise. "Do you know? I can't remember!" She slapped her hands on her knees as she counted back the days.

Mari laughed at her. "That would explain why you've been so tetchy lately..." she giggled at Yuriko's shock.

"I have not been tetchy!" the blonde insisted. She stopped for a moment, and considered. "All right, I have been. Am I really that bad - two weeks without "companionship" and I'm crawling out of my skin?" She caught the look in Mari's eyes.

"Yes," both women said simultaneously and laughed.

"Well," Yuriko stood and walked over to the closet, "that's easily rectified." She reached into the inner pocket of her jacket and pulled out a business card. Picking up the phone, she said over the mouthpiece to Mari, "I'm sorry, I won't be able to make dinner tomorrow with you and Hachi...I'll have a previous engagement." She smiled at the phone and asked for the waitress from the Chinese restaurant.

When Mari spoke, it was too soft for Yuriko to hear. "That's okay - Hachi and I weren't going out tomorrow anyway."

***

One Down, Two to Go

"Yes!" Yuriko held the paper triumphantly, waving it in Sayaka's face.

"Yes what?" The girl tried to glimpse what was written on the paper, but Yuriko was moving it around too fast to get a clear view.

Aya put her hand out to intercept the sheet as it passed and wrenched it from the blonde's grasp. She looked at the score and wrinkled her face up. "This is what you're happy about? Ugh. I wouldn't be able to show my face at home with a score like that."

Yuriko stuck her tongue out at her tutor. "Hey – I passed. That's great in my book."

Sayaka took the paper from Aya. "A seventy-six. Well, at least it's an improvement...." she said consolingly.

Aya made a rude noise. "Give me three more weeks and you'll be getting mid-eighties at least."

Yuriko stared at the girl in some surprise. "You're confident, aren't you?"

"Well, sure," Aya shot back at her. "You're not stupid – I can teach you anything, as long as you work at it. If you stick with me," Aya elbowed Yuriko in the arm, "you'll be getting A's in no time."

Yuriko's eyebrows rose. "You really think so?"

Aya nodded vigorously. "Definitely!"

Yuriko sat back down and looked at her Japanese test. A's, really? Then mentally slapped herself on her forehead. What the *hell* was she thinking?

***

The substitute for science class was an unremarkable middle-aged man, who felt that the best way to imbue young minds with a love for science was to drone endlessly on about scientific advances made by people he knew personally. He didn't seem to notice that a camera had been filming the class, nor when Namba gave it up as a bad job and took a break.

Yuriko stifled yet another yawn, clamping down on it hard enough to make her jaw hurt.

Okay, this was what she remembered high school as being – personal crises punctuated by intensely boring classes. She spent a moment feeling nostalgic, snorted and moved on.

***

The crowd today had grown to seven. Class leader Sato and a friend had joined the five girls for the lunchtime ritual. Sato's friend blew a fanfare into his fist as Yuriko unveiled today's offering. Neatly layered *yakitori*, a row of *tamago* and several decorated rice balls. The girls ooohed, while the boys tried to effect a trade. Yuriko declined, however, on the grounds that someone was going to a lot of trouble to feed her and who was she to deny them the pleasure?

She penned her usual note of thanks and tucked it inside the empty bentou box. She and the other girls were heading back towards the school when they heard the commotion.

As they rounded the corner, they came across a crowd milling about two girls - one on the ground, apparently unconscious. Yuriko forced her way through the crowd, accompanied by Sato and Mikan. When Yuriko knelt down to take a look at the girl on the ground, she was surprised to find

that it was Mie, her uber-fan from the writing club. Mikan took charge of Mie's friend, who appeared to be incoherent, soothing her with comforting words. Yuriko felt for a pulse and listened for breathing - both seemed to be fine. She turned to Sato and asked him to run to the clinic and let the doctor know she'd be bringing someone in. The boy ran off quickly. Yuriko lifted the fallen girl in her arms, and Mikan accompanied the other girl, who continued to babble hysterically.

As the four women walked to the clinic, Mikan was able to get the girl to tell them what had happened. Apparently she and Mie had been standing there laughing at something when Mie simply swayed in place and fell. Yuriko glanced down at Mie's pale face and reassured the girl that it was probably anemia or something like it. At this, the girl began to cry again, and Mikan put her arm around the girl's shoulders to soothe her.

Yuriko carried Mie into the clinic and was met at the door by the doctor of the school. She was an older woman, not inclined to panic, and Yuriko relaxed immediately. Seeing that Mie's breathing and blood pressure were steady, she asked Yuriko to watch the girl while she tended to her hysterical classmate. Yuriko pulled a chair up to the bed where Mie lay and watched the pale face for any signs of change. She could hear the doctor's deep voice, Mikan's solid tones, and the girl's own high-pitched wails, which eventually calmed, then stopped. She still sobbed, but her hysteria seemed to be receding. Yuriko was glad for that, at least.

After a quarter of an hour, Mikan appeared in front of Yuriko. "I have to get back to class. Asashi-sensei says that Chieko-san will be fine. She'll rest here for a while." Mikan looked down at the unconscious girl on the cot and back to Yuriko. "Should I let your teacher know where you are?"

Yuriko thanked Mikan profusely. "And let my PA know too - she's probably wondering where the hell I've gotten to."

"Namba-san has already told her." Mikan smiled. "He's a nice person, when you can get him talking."

Yuriko looked surprised. "Yeah, I guess so," she agreed. "But how did you get him talking? He's always so...professional with me."

"Oh, I asked him about his son." Mikan shot Yuriko a triumphant grin. Yuriko knew she was being set up, but played along.

"And how did you know to ask about his

Name: Sawako Ryuuichi

Birthday: April 30

Zodiac Sign: Taurus

Blood Type: AB

Occupation: Math Teacher

Favorite Color: Navy Blue

Favorite Food: Miso, Sushi

Favorite Music: Shamisen

Least Favorite Things: Lazy Students, Interruptions in Class

son?" Yuriko gave her the lead-in.

"He went to this school. Graduated two years ago...."

"That figures. And?" Yuriko could see that her "sempai" had yet another bit of insider knowledge.

"And," Mikan winked, acknowledging that she was cheating, "he went out with my sister for a year."

Yuriko nodded. "You learn something new every day." Mikan gave a little wave and left the clinic.

The doctor pulled the screen back and bent down to examine Mie more thoroughly. Yuriko stood and walked away, so the girl could have some privacy. The doctor spoke, while she listened to Mie's heartbeat and took the girl's pulse.

"Are you her friend?" The doctor's voice was low and a little gruff. "What is her name?"

"I'm not really a friend, her name is Mie, but I don't know her family name...or what class she's in. You might want to ask the other girl that came in with her - she's closer than I am, I think."

The doctor grunted slightly as she stood. Her eyes were sharp as she took in Yuriko's tall form. "You're not a student here - why are you in the school uniform?" She smiled to take the sting from her words.

Yuriko hastened to introduce herself and explain her situation.

The doctor smiled brightly. "Oh-ho! So you're the one that's causing all the ruckus," she chuckled to herself. "Hmph - I'm surprised we haven't had more fainting cases."

Yuriko smiled, uncertain if the doctor was making a joke or not.

"I'm Asashi, the school doctor. It's nice to make your acquaintance." The doctor introduced herself with an odd mixture of formality and familiarity. Yuriko bowed.

"Well, now," the doctor peered down at the sleeping girl. Some color had come back to her face. "I suppose I should go have the office call her parents. Would you mind terribly if I asked you to watch her until I get back? You don't seem the type to get hysterical if there's an emergency." The doctor's bright eyes flashed as she looked up towards the blonde. Yuriko had a strange sense about the woman, as if they'd met before.

"No," she reassured the older woman, "I'm not likely to get hysterical."

"Good." The doctor turned away brusquely and slid the screen back into place behind her. "If the other girl, um, Chieko-chan, wakes while I'm gone, send her back to class. She just needed to relax. A little high-strung."

"Okay." Yuriko said, but the doctor had already left. She looked down at Mie and thought how very, very young she looked like that. Fragile and vulnerable like a doll. Yuriko sighed and turned back to the window to wait until the doctor returned.

***

Volume 1, Issue 19

A Bitter Pill

Thirty minutes had passed. The doctor had been in and out twice. Chieko had gone back to class, but still Yuriko sat, watching the sleeping form on the bed. She didn't even *like* Mie, why did she care if she was well? This question kept popping into Yuriko's thoughts so regularly she considered setting her watch by it.

"Why?" she asked the sleeping girl softly.

Mie stirred and moaned a little. Yuriko stiffened as the girl's eyes opened and she asked sleepily, "Why what?" Mie blinked, and looked around, clearly puzzled.

"Do you know where you are?" Yuriko asked, ignoring Mie's question.

"No." The girl struggled to sit up, but Yuriko held her down with a light hand on her shoulder.

"Don't try to get up. You're in the clinic, the doctor will be right back - she's gone to try and contact your parents. What's the last thing you remember?"

Mie's eyes roamed, trying to fix her thoughts. "I was standing outside...talking to Chieko-chan...."

Yuriko nodded. "Right. Good. And you passed out. Do you remember anything about that?"

"No," Mie said, then immediately rescinded the comment. "Wait, I remember talking to Chieko-chan and I was dizzy...but that's all I remember."

Yuriko let go of the breath she'd been holding. "That's alright. You remember everything, then. Can you think of a reason why you'd pass out so suddenly?" This last was more of a rhetorical question, so Yuriko was surprised to get an answer at all.

"I do, sometimes. Never at school before, though." Mie's eyes were clear, Yuriko noted, and very large. She looked more like a doll awake than she had asleep.

The girl caught Yuriko's eyes with her own, and her face colored a little. "Have you been here long with me?" she asked.

Yuriko realized that her hand still lay on the girl's shoulder and pulled it away quickly. "About an hour." Her voice was sharper than she had intended.

"I'm sorry for being such an inconvenience," Mie began, then stopped suddenly. "How's Chieko-chan? She gets very excited by things happening suddenly...."

Yuriko waved Mie's concern away. "She was a little upset, but she's back in class now." She watched as the girl relaxed, then drew in a little breath. Yuriko had an unpleasant feeling in her stomach as she watched the emotions flit across Mie's face - and realized why she had stayed. *Better get this over with now,* she thought. But she wasn't very happy with herself at the moment.

Mie reached out and hesitantly took Yuriko's hand with her own. "Thank you for caring about me, for staying with me." The girl's cheeks flushed, and Yuriko swallowed the bile that rose up in her throat at what she was about to do.

"Yuriko-sama," Mie blurted, "I love you! I know I'm young, but I really love you - I have since I first saw you." Her voice dropped to a whisper. "I know...everyone knows you like girls and that you don't have a girl-friend...."

Yuriko couldn't stand it. "Please stop," she said gruffly, her voice hoarse. "Please." She pulled her hand from the girl's grasp. "I'm sorry, Mie-san." She wished she could remember the girl's family name. "I really am. You're a lovely child and you'll find someone to love soon. But not me, not now. So please don't."

"But..." Mie pleaded, her eyes filling with tears.

Yuriko loathed herself that moment, knowing that she was about to alienate a fan, a schoolmate, a nice girl, but not seeing any other way to handle it. "I don't love you, Mie-san. I can't love you back. I'm sorry."

Tears began to flow from Mie's eyes as the girl sat up. "Please, don't leave!" She threw her arms around Yuriko's neck, embracing her tightly. Yuriko could feel a hot cheek pressed against her neck, and the trickle of tears. She disentangled herself from the girl and stood.

"Don't. You don't know what you're asking, what you're saying." Yuriko's voice was harsh. "You can't know." She clamped down on the cruelties that made their way to her lips. Turning on her heels she said, "I hope you feel better soon," and walked out of the clinic.

Feeling ill, Yuriko walked down the hallway, not noticing where she was headed. When she found herself facing the front entrance of the school she paused for a moment, then walked outside without a second thought.

***

Yuriko wandered off the school grounds, her mood as foul as any she had felt in a long time. It wasn't often she had to do that, but every time it left a terrible taste in her mouth. Why couldn't fans be content with what they were given?

She regretted wearing the girl's uniform today; the pockets were inadequate for her needs. She could hardly stuff her hands in them and walk. What the hell did girls do with their hands when they were miserable? She thought back to scenes from her high school days...oh, right, they clutched things. She clenched her fists and kept walking.

On a pedestrian bridge she paused to watch the traffic go by. The noise was soothing, rather like an uneven river of sound. She leaned on the cement rail, and went over the scene in the clinic, wondering if she could have been gentler, or firmer, or... the thoughts wheeled around in her head, dizzying her.

"It never gets any easier, does it?" she murmured to herself, heedless of the people passing by, staring at her.

A hand on her arm drew her attention back to the real world. A middle-aged man, about her height, had clamped his hand around her arm. He squeezed as he talked.

"Shouldn't you be in school?" his voice was insinuating.

Yuriko was disgusted - she jerked her arm out of his grasp, drew herself up to her full height and looked down her nose at him. "No. I'm engaging in an entirely private fetish for wearing sailor suits - you might try it, it's a damn sight less harmful than your schoolgirl fetish." Ignoring the look on the man's face, or the obscenities that sprung from his lips, she began to walk away, her mood even blacker than before. A jerk on her arm spun her around, and the slap across her face paralyzed her with shock.

"You little bitch! If you don't come with me, I'll report you to your school. We'll see who has the fetish!" The man's eyes bulged and his lips peeled back in a sneer. Yuriko hauled on her arm, but his grip was strong. She was about to kick him when a voice interrupted.

"Uh, mister...unless you want to be beaten silly, you'd better let go of her." The man spun around, but didn't let go of Yuriko's arm. So startled was she that she forgot to try and free herself.

"What?" the man fumed. "You think you can take me, punk?"

"Well, the four of us should be able to." A second voice came from behind Yuriko, and she turned, this time remembering to recover her arm and step away from the man, who now found himself surrounded by four threatening figures. One swung a bicycle chain nonchalantly, while another held a small, hand-sized *tonfa*. A third young thug, whose short stocky frame and peering eyes made him seem more threatening than he was, stepped up and pulled Yuriko possessively towards himself.

"Old man, next time you want some afternoon fun, you keep your hands off my girl." The stocky boy faked a move in the man's direction and he jumped. The boy laughed nastily. He nodded to the others. "Go ahead, teach him a lesson." The three advanced on the man, who broke and ran away.

Yuriko watched him run off and slowly let herself relax. After a moment, she turned to Uto and slapped him across the chest.

"Idiot! What the hell are you doing out here?"

Uto laughed. "You're welcome, Yuri-chan." He waved his gang back, as they approached. Togai stepped quickly up to Yuriko and asked if she was alright. "He didn't do anything to you, did he?" Togai's concern was really touching and Yuriko said as much.

"No, I'm fine, just having a bad day." She rubbed her temples, then smacked Uto again, this time with a little energy behind it. "Jerk. 'My girl' indeed!"

The gang leader just grinned insolently at her. "Lucky for me you were in drag today, or the guy would've thought I was a fag."

Yuriko grinned at this, then began to laugh. "What an asshole he was. Thanks for the rescue. He was in real danger of me kicking the shit out of him." Her face fell as she thought of why she was playing hooky. To draw attention away from herself, she pointed to Ni-ru, who was tucking the chain into his pocket, and Heiji, who was twirling the tonfa around his fingers. "You guys do the tough act really well. Good thing I'm the only one who knows you're a bunch of pussies."

Ni-ru flashed his gap-toothed grin at her. "Yeah, well, girls like "sensitive" guys, don't they?"

"Ugh." Yuriko said emphatically. "I really don't want to talk about girls right now."

Uto's eyebrow rose. "No? Why not?" He paused, reflecting. "It couldn't be that our little Yuri-chan was rejected, was she?" He shot her a squinting glance.

"No!" Yuriko insisted. "No, I had to blow someone off this afternoon."

"Oh," Togai empathized, with no real understanding. "That sucks."

"Yeah." Yuriko looked around at the boys and made a decision. "I owe you one...although I would have been able to handle it myself, thank you very much...how about I buy you all a coffee?"

"Beer?" Heiji asked.

"Coffee," Yuriko insisted with a wry grin. "Come on, my treat."

As the five walked off, Yuriko thought to herself that school life was a lot bizarrer this time around than she remembered it.

***

The Persistence of the Surreal

Yuriko poured out two glasses of wine, smiling the whole time. She handed one of the glasses to the other woman, murmured a soft toast and they drank.

Hikari had the most delightful smile, Yuriko noted. She said as much, prompting that same smile to appear once again. Yuriko spent a moment letting her glance linger on the woman's lips and turned to the menu. This was, she thought, exactly what she needed...on more than one level.

Her date was voluptuous by Japanese standards, and Yuriko was fascinated with the way her dress moved over her curves, watching both openly and covertly. The woman exuded a kind of comfortable sensuality that fascinated Yuriko. Like so many hostesses who used their body language to speak of unspeakable things, this woman's every gesture was eloquent. Yuriko looked forward to a long discussion with her.

The restaurant was not crowded; it was still early in the evening. The quiet atmosphere gave them a sense of intimacy that heightened the enjoyment of their flirtation. Yuriko gave a soft purr as the other woman ran her tongue lightly across her bottom lip, ostensibly to lick up a drop of wine that had escaped.

Appetizers came, and were promptly ignored. Yuriko was hungry, but not for food. She toyed with the fish on her plate, drawing out the meaningless chatter and small-talk behind which both women were conversing on far, far more important issues.

Hikari laughed, a husky, melodic laugh, and Yuriko could feel a thrill run along her spine. This was the kind of voice she loved to hear moaning in her ear in bed. As if she had read Yuriko's mind, Hikari mentioned, almost casually, that she thought they might have dessert at her place, if that was okay with Yuriko. It was most definitely okay with Yuriko.

The two women spoke of inconsequentials as dinner arrived. A smoldering look from over a forkful of fine cuisine and this time it was Hikari who purred.

Yuriko washed her hands in the ladies room, ran her hand through her hair. A touch along her back brought her focus on the mirror to the woman behind her. Hikari let her hand trail along Yuriko's back and arm as she walked past the blonde. Yuriko openly watched her date walk into a stall, enjoying the subtle ebb and flow of her dress. The blonde sighed with great satisfaction, and stepped to the door.

"I'll be waiting outside," Yuriko said as she let the door close behind her. She paid the bill and went to retrieve their coats, waiting for Hikari to join her. As she stood in the foyer of the restaurant she heard, "Yuriko-kun!" followed immediately by several surprised exclamations of, "Yuriko-san!" She turned away from the coat check to see the girl's basketball team entering the restaurant. Surprised, she asked them what they were doing here, and was informed that they were celebrating a big win in tonight's game.

"Congratulations!" Yuriko said with sincerity. "That's great!" She caught Mikan's eye, "So you didn't need me after all, eh?" The girls laughed. The maitre d' approached and announced that the girls' table was ready. Several of the girls insisted Yuriko join them for the celebration. Yuriko tried to decline, but two firm grips took hold of her wrists. Yuriko was casting her glance around for her date as she was dragged towards the large back room, until a cold voice broke up the scene.

"Leave her alone." Yuriko's wrists were immediately released and the crowd turned towards the latecomer. Yamamoto Kaori looked at Yuriko with disdain. "She obviously doesn't want to be disturbed."

Mikan laughed and clapped Yamamoto on the shoulder. "Oh, come *on*, Buchou! Lighten up!"

Yuriko straightened her cuffs and cleared her throat. Kaori had never let her gaze waiver from Yuriko's face, nor was there any change in her mien as the team captain spoke. "Mikan, don't be a fool. Can't you see she's out on a date?" Disapproval, while not actually voiced, was implicit in the girl's comment.

Mikan pulled back from the captain sharply and glanced at Yuriko, who muttered an apology. The team vice-captain blushed as she tried to apologize for interrupting Yuriko's evening.

The blonde waved the apologies away and made her way back through the group, towards the door. With much bowing and apologies on both sides, Yuriko made her escape at last. Back in the lobby, she found a distinctly annoyed-looking Hikari. As she was helped on with her coat, the hostess asked, "Who were those girls? And why were they dragging you off?" Her sense of humor had returned, and Yuriko grinned at her.

"It might make a good bedtime story," she said and held her arm out for the other woman to take. "If you're a good girl."

Name: Noda Mikan

Birthday: March 25

Zodiac Sign: Aries

Blood Type: O

Occupation: Vice-Captain of the Basketball Team

Favorite Color: Blue

Favorite Food: Crepes

Favorite Music: Whatever's on the radio

Least Favorite Things: None

"Oh," Hikari rejoined, taking the proffered arm. "I'm always good."

Yuriko laughed, and the two women left the restaurant.

***

Yuriko ran her eyes along the CD rack in Hikari's apartment; popular music, a few well-known Enka singers...the selection was unremarkable. She poured out two glasses of wine and squatted to see the rest of the CDs. One caught her attention and she quickly pulled it out, her eyebrow raised. Her lower lip pushed out with interest. She stood and turned on the CD player, slipping the disc in and turning the volume down. The opening notes of a string quartet began to play. Yuriko seated herself on the sofa and closed her eyes, while the quartet broke into four separate threads, melodic and discordant all at once.

"You like Biber?" Hikari asked, coming back into the room. "Not many people do."

"I like interesting music." Yuriko sat forward and smiled at the hostess. She had changed into a silk *yukata* and, as with her dress, the material moved delightfully across her curves. "I like interesting things...and people."

Hikari came around the couch and placed a tray of strawberries on the table. She picked one off the tray and took a delicate bite. Pushing Yuriko backwards until she reclined on the sofa once again, Hikari seated herself across Yuriko's lap and held the bitten strawberry up for Yuriko to taste. The blonde did, with dispatch, her eyes on Hikari's mouth the entire time.

The hostess finished the strawberry, picked up a second one and once again, fed it to Yuriko. Black hair fell across Hikari's arm, and she moved to brush it away, but Yuriko was there first. Gently, she brushed the hair back from the waitress' arm, then followed the hair upwards, sliding her hand under Hikari's head. Placing a slight pressure on her neck, Yuriko leaned forward, the strawberry still caught between her teeth.

Hikari placed her mouth on the strawberry and bit off half, her lips brushing Yuriko's. Smiling against the woman's mouth, Yuriko kept her hand on Hikari, tangling her hand in the luxurious black hair and kissing the woman. Hikari responded without hesitation, opening her mouth to Yuriko, allowing tongue and strawberry to mix.

Yuriko brought her other hand up to claim Hikari's shoulder, drawing the woman into her. Their kissing took on more urgency. Hikari took Yuriko's face in her hands, placing kisses all across the blonde's mouth, then licking at the corners with her strawberry-scented tongue.

After a few minutes they pulled away. Yuriko reached for a glass of wine and passed it to Hikari, who sipped at it, smiling from under hooded eyes. Yuriko picked up her own glass and clinked it against the waitress'.

"You know," Yuriko said, as Hikari fed her another strawberry, "you make an excellent dessert."

Hikari laughed. "You mean I'll make an excellent dessert."

Yuriko nodded and drew the other woman closer. "Exactly." She leaned forward and kissed Hikari's throat at the base, then worked her way up to the curve of her jaw. Lightly, she bit into the other woman's neck and again, when she heard the moan that came from her, Yuriko slid one hand under the collar of the yukata, feeling the soft shoulder, down to the curve of breast. Following her hand with kisses, she could feel Hikari put both hands around her neck. Yuriko untied the belt to the robe, allowing it to fall away from the voluptuous body on her lap.

Taking Hikari in both arms, Yuriko stood and, without taking her mouth away from the hostess' body, carried her into the bedroom, where they decided to have the rest of their dessert.

***

Volume 1, Issue 21

On the Seventh Day

Yuriko was awakened by soft breath blowing into her ear, followed by the brush of lips across her earlobe. As a tongue began to explore the area just below her ear, she moaned. A soft laugh seemed loud from proximity and she rolled over to smile into the face of Hikari. As that lovely smile filled the woman's face. Yuriko completely forgot her sleepiness and embraced the luscious waitress for a lingering good-morning kiss.

Hikari broke away, lowering her head to Yuriko's chest, and the blonde found herself lost in conflicting sensations. Her back arched as Hikari began to suck on her, while one hand found its way between her legs. Yuriko pulled herself towards the brunette as pleasure brushed away any last cobwebs of sleep. When at last she relaxed back onto the bed, and Hikari's soft hair covered her body like a blanket, the waitress whispered, "Good morning."

Yuriko put one arm behind her head and returned the greeting. "A very good morning to you." They lay there for some time, while Yuriko drifted in and out of sleep. When she woke up for the last time, Hikari was lying on her chest, one hand curled under her chin like a child, asleep. Yuriko tugged on the curled hand, drawing it up to her mouth. Fair was fair, she thought, as she began to kiss each finger, sliding her tongue between them.

***

Yuriko kissed the waitress before leaving the apartment, and they promised to get together again. No date was set, no unkeepable commitments were made, but there was no doubt in either of their minds that they would see each other again. Yuriko caught a cab back to her apartment, grinning the whole way home.

The phone was ringing as she opened the door. Yuriko picked up it before closing the door behind her.

"Yeh-llo!" Yuriko's voice was chipper. Laughter was the only response, and she said acerbically, "Good morning, Mari."

"Good afternoon, Yuri," her friend responded without missing a beat. "That answers my first question."

"And your second?" Yuriko poured herself a glass of orange juice and drank as Mariko spoke.

"Wondering whether you're booked for the studio today or I can borrow your impeccable fashion sense for nefarious purposes."

"I'm all yours. Uh, provided I get a meal out of this. I haven't eaten breakfast yet." Glancing at the clock, she continued, "Or lunch."

"Meet me at the 24/7 in half an hour." Mari didn't bother hiding the snicker in her voice. "You can eat whatever you like, my treat. Food, that is."

Yuriko rung off. "My goodness - that girl is so arch, she's practically Roman," she commented to the room at large.

***

Yuriko was waiting for Mariko, when the other woman showed up, twenty minutes late. One look at her friend and Yuriko knew something was wrong. She let several minutes pass in silence as they took their seats and ordered. When their food arrived and still Mari hadn't said anything, Yuriko pushed.

"Okay, what's up?" Yuriko said over her coffee. "And don't tell me nothing. I'm not blind and you're a bad liar."

Mari looked away. "Just some problems with Hachi. He's been working late all week and..." She looked unhappily at her omelet.

"And?" Yuriko set the coffee down.

"And we had a fight about it." Mari pushed the food around on her plate, mixing eggs and hot sauce into a impressionistic mass. "He had to cancel our dinner last night." Yuriko's eyebrows rose at this - their Saturday night date had become a fixed point in their schedule. "And he just called to say that he wouldn't be able to make dinner with my family this week." Mari met Yuriko's gaze, and the blonde was surprised to see her friend's eyes fill with tears.

"It's only for a little while, though, right?" Yuriko asked soothingly.

Mari shrugged. "That's what he says, but...but what if it isn't? What if this is just a glimpse of what the future will be?" Mari reached across the table and gripped Yuriko's wrist. "Yuri - I don't want to be married to a salary-man who lives for his job. You know I don't!" Her voice sounded desperate.

Yuriko placed her free hand on Mariko's. "Don't you think you're being a little hasty?" She spoke softly. "I mean, this is his first big break - give the guy a chance...."

Mari shook her head anxiously. "No, there's something else. I can't tell you what, but I know there's something else. He's lying to me about something. And I don't know what it is." Mariko lost her grip and began to sob. "I love him so much! I don't want to lose him!"

Yuriko took both her friend's hands in hers and squeezed them. "I've known Hachi almost as long as I've known you. If he's lying to you, I'll find out what it's all about, okay?"

Mari her tear-streaked face miserable and childlike, looked at the blonde. Slowly she nodded.

"I'm sure it's something silly - like what he's getting you as a wedding present." Yuriko smiled reassuringly, as Mari wiped the tears from her face.

"You're probably right," Mari said bravely, sniffling a little. "I don't know why I'm worried." She took a deep shuddering breath. "But I have the most awful feeling about it...."

Yuriko frowned. Mari's premonitions were, more often than not, correct. If she felt something bad, they'd both best be prepared for the worst. And they both knew it. She gave Mariko's hand a final squeeze.

"Whatever happens, we'll always be there for each other, right?" Mariko asked.

Yuriko gave her friend a look. "Of course we will. What a silly thing to say!"

Mari made a face. "It's not like we've been close the past few weeks."

Yuriko was struck by the simple comment. It robbed her of breath. "Oh, my gods, Mari," she whispered at last. "Here I was, buried in homework, while you needed me." All of a sudden, Yuriko was angry at this ridiculous role she had to play. "That's it! I'm calling Kishi-san and telling her that I quit!" She disengaged a hand and reached into her pocket for her cell phone, but Mari reached out and stopped her.

"No! No - that's not what I meant...." Mariko gave her lips a tiny quirk. "You are so impossibly impulsive." She shook her head at her friend.

"But you're right." Yuriko insisted. "This stupid show has sucked my life away."

"Has it?" Mariko asked quietly. Yuriko glanced at her quizzically. "Well, think about it. You're making new friends - real ones, not just fans - you're more active physically than you've been in years, someone is feeding you better than usual," Mari's irrepressible grin reasserted itself at that, "and you've been writing poetry again." Mari's eyebrow lifted. "Ah - you thought I didn't notice, did you?" Mari tapped her nose. "I see everything - I know everything."

"You bribe my housecleaner." Yuriko drew herself back, pretending an offense she didn't feel. Sipping at her now-lukewarm coffee, Yuriko made a face and motioned the waitress for a refill.

Mari giggled and Yuriko relaxed. "Has the cleaner actually come yet?"

"No. This afternoon, supposedly. Would you believe," the blonde said with heavy irony, "they are actually sending a kid from Mitsukawa? What are the chances of that?"

Mari considered. "You said that Kishi-san arranged for this?"

Yuriko looked surprised. "Yeah, why?"

Mari gave her a knowing look. "I bet she did it on purpose."

Yuriko blinked. Then blinked again. "That conniving old...you're right, she probably did."

The two women laughed, then drank from their refilled cups. Silence fell between them as they ate their tepid meals.

As they left, Mariko said quickly, almost shyly, "You meant what you said - you'll ask Hachi?"

Yuriko nodded emphatically. "But, really, I bet it's just stress at work. You'll see - everything will be fine." She smiled at her friend, who gave her an unsure smile in return.

As they left the restaurant, Yuriko filled her friend in on the end to her extremely surreal week. She could at least guarantee that - she'd make sure she told Mariko everything that happened in her life, so she didn't feel out of the loop. Yuriko vowed to make sure she didn't neglect Mari, whatever went on in her life.

Volume 1, Issue 22

A Harbinger of Winter

By the time Mariko and Yuriko finished their raids on the shops of the *Ginza*, it was decided by both of them that it had been a well-deserved little slice of hedonism. Mariko had bought several pairs of new shoes, a dress (that had raised Yuriko's eyebrows very high indeed, and prompted a comment about Hachi and his comeuppance) and a coat for the colder weather. Yuriko had contented herself with a silk blouse and a new jacket, but in no way did she feel as if she had come out behind in the race.

Laughing, they deposited their bags in the hall of Mari's apartment as they removed their shoes.

"Did you see the look on that salesclerk's face when I bought the tie?" Mariko snickered. "I thought she was going to choke!"

Yuri grinned at her mischievous friend. "You know that's mean, playing with the saleshelp like that."

"I don't know what you mean," Mariko said innocently. "Just because I referred to you as my husband..." Mari laughed. "I just hate those stuck-up girls in the shops. They act like they do us a favor by selling us things. I didn't like the way they were looking at us."

"I know, I know," Yuriko said. "I know *exactly* how you feel about them - and so do they, now," she said sardonically.

Mari turned to look at her. "You weren't embarrassed, were you?" She peered hard at Yuriko, scrutinizing her friend closely. "You never used to get embarrassed when I did things like that."

Yuriko tugged on the hair that fell in front of her eyes in irritation. "I'm not embarrassed."

"Liar," Mariko shot back.

Yuriko blew out an exasperated breath. "It's not a lie - it's just that...what if..." her voice faded.

"What?" Mari demanded.

Yuriko turned away and shoved her hands in her pockets. She took a deep breath and let it out. "Don't hit me." She turned around and faced her friend with an embarrassed grin. "I was *going* to say, 'what if one of my classmates saw you?'"

Mari stared at Yuriko for a moment, put down the tea cup she held, walked calmly over to the blonde and smacked her lightly on the chest. Without a word, she turned back to the kitchen area, picked the teacup up and resumed wiping it dry.

Yuriko watched Mariko, and thought about all the many things, good and bad, that they'd been through, and smiled. Mari looked up and, catching the smile, sent back one of her own.

"You're getting old, Yuri," Mariko said, affectionately.

"Don't I know it."

"And grumpy."

"Agreed."

"And conservative."

"Hey! Wait a second! I'll accept the others, but not that."

Mari walked into the living room with a tea tray. "Okay, I rescind it. But only on the basis that I owe you one from this morning."

Yuriko shook her head as she sat. Mariko poured tea for both of them. "Am I really getting conservative?"

Mariko shrugged. "Probably not by other people's standards." She took a sip of tea as she considered. "Am I a worrywort?"

"No."

"Then you're not conservative."

They drank in silence for a few moments. Yuriko placed her cup on the saucer, folded her hands together and sighed. "I feel...ugh...responsible for these kids."

"I know," Mariko replied calmly. "That's the way you've always been. When you meet new people, whether they like you or not, you feel responsible for them. You care very much about people. Not like me."

Yuri glanced at the other woman. "No, you care, but in a different way - deeper, more personally."

"Umm," Mari said noncommittally.

Yuriko glanced at her watch, which had beeped quietly. "I have to go - the new cleaner's coming, and I have an engagement tonight."

"Going dancing again? On a school night?"

Nodding, Yuriko stood. "Well, Ruriko-sensei is new at the whole thing. She's not sure where to go yet. Plus, she asked me to be her dance partner until she...well, you know. Anyway, we have to fit time into both our schedules, so..."

"Well, have fun!" Mariko accompanied her friend to the door. As if the thought had just occured to her, she asked, "Hey - can I come with you next time?" She twirled as she spoke. "I'm not a bad dancer myself."

Yuriko laughed as she slipped her shoes on. "Sure, but remember, you'll have to lead!"

Mari stuck her tongue out. "Not if I find myself a handsome butch as a dance partner," she teased.

Yuriko pretended to fluff up her feathers. "Wait a second - you already *have* a handsome butch dance partner!"

Mari nodded, "Just checking."

Yuriko leaned over the step up to the apartment and kissed Mariko on the cheek. "Tuesday at 8:30 - get dolled up."

Mariko waved as Yuriko opened the door to leave. "I'll be in my new dress."

Yuriko turned, her eyes wide. "That'll definitely get you a dance partner," she exclaimed, and closed the door on her friend's laughter.

***

The doorbell rang. Yuriko shuffled out to to greet her new housekeeper. She wondered if Kishi-san would have arranged for a cute, but easily distracted girl, or a plainer, more competent one. She made a bet with herself for the latter and glanced through the peephole. Distorted by the curved lens, she could make out huge eyes framed by long soft eyelashes, a delicate nose and a pair of the most beautiful lips she'd ever seen. Yuriko opened the door with a slight bow.

The voice that responded to her was soft, and the hair as the figure bowed was long and flowing. When the figure stood, she was surprised to note that it was actually male. The boy was unbelievably beautiful - a classic *bishounen*; narrow waist, slight build, he was nearly her own height, with full lips and deep eyes that were simply captivating. Yuriko realized she was staring and invited the boy in.

Haltingly, unable to stop looking at him, she introduced herself and welcomed him in. Those deep eyes considered her for a moment before he spoke.

"I'm Ishida, Ryo Ishida. Nice to meet you." There was a quirk in his mouth that belied the sorrow in his eyes. She also noted that he had given his name Western style.

Yuriko pondered the name. "I've met you before, haven't I?" She shook her head as she led the young man into her apartment. "I'm sorry - I'm usually very good with names and faces, but."

"We weren't actually introduced formally. I'm in the art club - I was there for the leaf viewing."

Yuriko gestured. "That was it. Your sketch was very good, if I remember correctly."

Ryo waved the compliment away. "It wasn't that good."

Yuriko rounded on him, affecting a fierce demeanor. "Let's get this straight, in my house I am the law. If I say you're good..."she left the rest of the sentence unfinished.

Ryo bowed contritely, but as he stood upright, that little quirk reappeared at the corner of his mouth. "Of course."

Yuriko gazed at him for a moment more, shook her head and turned towards the room at large. She gestured broadly. "I don't know what you were actually hired to do, but with the exception of those piles," she pointed to the table and stopped. "Ryo." She turned to the boy and, with her hands on her hips, demanded, "You wrote that note, didn't you?"

The boy turned red, but held her gaze. "I'm surprised you remember it. You must have received," he glanced at the tall piles of notes, and corrected his tense, "are receiving, a lot of them."

"Yours stood out, for several reasons."

"Oh?" Ryo clearly wasn't the type to give anything away. They looked at each other for a long moment, taking each other's measure. Yuriko made a sudden decision.

"Did you take this job out of curiosity, or do you need the money?" she asked suddenly.

Ryo looked nonplussed. "I, that is..."

Yuriko waved away his fudging. "Be honest."

"I need the money." Ryo's chin jutted out with pride. "I want to go to art school, but my parents won't pay for that. so...."

"Fine." Yuriko said. "You're hired."

Continued Online

www.yuricon.com/shoujoai-ni-bouken/

Glossary of Terms and Concepts

Honorifics - Endings on Japanese names that denote the relationship between the speaker and the one spoken to.

-san is added to any name as a general rule when there is no special relationship. Often translated as "Mr." "Miss," "Mrs." or "Ms." as appropiate, "-san" is the most commonly used honorific

-chan is used for young children, girls, and often by female friends well into adulthood.

-kun is used for boys, especially classmates; or for subordinates in a business setting.

-sama is rarely used in normal life. It is an expression of great respect, used for the Royal Family - and sometimes by fans towards their idol.

-sensei means "teacher." It is used to address teachers, writers and doctors.

-buchou is used to address school club presidents or, in the business world, division managers.

School Terms and Concepts

School Uniforms
Students in junior high and high school may wear school uniforms. Boy's uniforms (like the one in this novel) were originally patterned after military uniforms, with a high stiff collar, and girl's uniforms may have sailor collars.

Shoe Lockers
Students do not have lockers, in the American sense. They change their outside shoes for inside slippers in small lockers near the school entrance.

Teachers
Students usually stay in one classroom for the duration of the school day, while the teachers for the various subjects come to them.

Sempai/Kouhai
Older and more experienced students, called *sempai*, will mentor younger, less

experienced students, called *kouhai*. This relationship can often last long after graduation.

Day Duty
Students are responsible for cleaning their classrooms. Classes share cleaning duties on shared rooms, like the music room.

School on Saturday
Although this is less common now, many Japanese schools have classes on Saturdays.

General Terms and Concepts

Names
Japanese names are written and spoken as Family Name then Given Name, as in our bios - i.e, Hayashi Mariko.

Blood Types
Like zodiac signs, blood types are considered to be indicators of personality. Type O are extroverted leaders, Type A are organized and a hard workers, Type B are individualist and stubborn, and Type AB are aloof and controlled.

Love Hotel
Love Hotels are inexpensive short-stay hotels that are favored by couples looking for a private place to be intimate.

Bentou
A bentou is a boxed lunch, usually made up of an assortment of small dishes, accompanied by rice. Bentou are very popular for lunch.

Bishounen
A pretty boy.

Furo
A Japanese bath, usually deeper and larger than American baths

Furoshiki
Patterned cloth used to wrap up any variety of objects, including *bentou* boxes.

Ginza
High-end shopping district in Tokyo.

Haiku
Form of poetry, of three lines of five, seven and five syllables.

Kampai
is a toast, like "cheers."

Tamago
Sweet folded egg omelet, sometimes on sushi rice.

Tonfa
Similar to a police nightstick, a tonfa is a common weapon in Okinawan martial arts.

Yakitori
Grilled chicken strips on skewers

Yukata
A light, informal kimono for summer and house wear.

Looking for stories where the girl *always* gets the girl? Try 100% yuri manga from

ALC Publishing

Yuri Monogatari
Rica 'tte Kanji!?
WORKS

Available through the following distributors:

Diamond Comics
Planet Anime   W&G Foyles (UK)
Animenation   AnimeCastle.com
Little Sister's Bookstore   Alamo Square Distributors

ALC Shop
http://www.anilesbocon.org/shop/